WHITE MAGICK

High Witchcraft
Complete Formulary

First published in French by Unicursal under the title:
Magie Blanche: Formulaire Complet de Haute Sorcellerie.

Éditions Unicursal Publishers
unicursal.ca

ISBN 978-2-89806-299-5 (PB)
ISBN 978-2-89806-300-8 (HC)

First English Edition, Beltane 2022

WHITE MAGICK

High Witchcraft
Complete Formulary

M-A RICARD

UNICURSAL

TABLE OF CONTENT

Prologue 15
Introduction 19

FIRST PART

The Awakening of the Witch

Pure & Simple Magick 25
Do we have to be initiated to become a Witch ? 31
A Tradition in Harmony with Nature 35
Low Magick or High Magick ? 39
The Witches' Rede & Fundamental Principles 43
    The 20 Fundamental Principles of Witchcraft 46
Karma : Law of Incarnations & Triple Return 49
How to Effectively Formulate Requests During Rituals . 55
Acquiring Witches' Magickal Powers 61
    Will 63
    Visualization 65
    Intuition 67
    Faith 70
    Meditation 71
    The Sense of Mystery : Silence 74
The Power of the Verb & Incantations 79

SECOND PART
Preliminary Preparations

Choosing Your Witch's Name 85

The Witches' Alphabet 91

Ceremonial Clothes 95

Witches' Personal Jewels 99

Magickal Tools of the Trade 103

　　The Altar 106

　　The Athame 110

　　The Bolline 113

　　The Cup or Chalice 115

　　The Pentacle 116

　　The Censer or Incense Burner 119

　　The Cauldron 120

　　The Candleholders 121

　　The Book of Shadows and the Quill Pen 123

　　The Magick Wand 126

　　The Sword 130

　　The Bell 131

　　Bowls of Water and Salt 131

The Cingulum . . . .

　　131 Exorcisms & Consecrations of Magickal Tools . .133

　　Consecration Formula of Water and Salt 135

　　Exorcism Formula 136

　　Athame Consecration Formula 137

　　Wand Consecration and Charge Formula 139

　　Consecration Formula for Other Tools 141

　　Notes about consecrating Magickal Tools 143

Magick Circles: Power Lenses 145

Three Types of Magic Circles 147
Casting the Magick Circles 150
Closing and Sending the Circle back to the Universe 155

THIRD PART
Initiation to Witchcraft & Universal Vibrations

The Great God Cernunnos Invocation 159
The Charge of the Goddess 161
Solitary Initiation to Witchcraft 163
    Preliminary preparations 165
The Initiation Ritual. .166
The Secret of Magickal Baths & of the Purification of
    Bodies 171
    Purifying Immersions 173
    The Quick Shower. 174
    Magnetic Immersions 175
    Example of a Magick Bath Ritual 179
The use of Light & Magick Lamps 183
    Types of Magickal Correspondences Associated
    with Colors. 185
    The Vibratory Correspondences 185
    Psychological Correspondences. 187
    The Use of Candles in Witchcraft. 189
    The True Magickal and Vibratory Correspondences
    of Colors 191
Of the Magickal Use of Incense & Fumigations 197
    The Occult Properties of Incense 198
    Method of preparation of Incenses 201

Basic Incenses 204
Sabbatical Incense Recipes 208
Plant Compositions for Magick Baths and Incense. . . .211
Purification and Exorcism. 213
Protection 216
Psychism and Psychic Powers 219
Money and Wealth. 222
Work and Social Elevation. 225
Love and Feelings 228
Health, Peace and Well-Being. 233
Strength and Power 238
Prosperity, Luck and Success 241

FOURTH PART
Harmonizing with Cycles, Time & Cosmos

Days of Power, Lunar Cycles & Seasons. 247
Lunar Phases and Cycles 249
The Influences and Correspondences of the Planetary Spheres 255
Calculation of Planetary Hours 259
The Sabbaths: Witches' Festivals 265
Samhain 269
Yule – Winter Solstice 272
Imbolg. 275
Ostara — Spring Equinox. 278
Beltane. 281
Litha — Summer Solstice 284
Lughnasadh 287
Mabon — Autumn Equinox. 290

FIFTH PART
Magickal Consciousness

Familiars 295
    The Familiars of the Animal Kingdom 296
    How to create your own Familiars 299
    Familiar's Technical Sheet 305
Ritual of the Familiar 307
Divination Techniques. 311
    Magic Mirror Divination 313
    Tarot Divination 315
    Divinatory Technique by the Major Arcana. 318
    Example of divination 320
    Divinatory Meaning of the Major Arcana. 323
Rituals in Practical Magick 327
    The Dynamics of Rituals. 329
    How to Create Rituals: The Eleven Rules to Follow .332
Ritual Outline for Practical Witchcraft 340

SIXTH PART
The Grimoire of the Earth

Ritual Practice 345
Ritual of Purification and Exorcism. 347
Ritual of Protection 350
Ritual of Psychism and Psychic Powers 354
Ritual of Money and Wealth. 358
Ritual of Work and Social Elevation. 362
Ritual of Love and Feelings 366

Ritual of Health, Peace and Well-being 369
Ritual of Strength and Power 372
Ritual of Prosperity, Luck and Success 376

The Virtues of Herbs, Plants & Essential Oils 381

PLATES, CHARACTERS & SYMBOLS

The Witches' Alphabet 92
Tau Robe/Simple Tabard 97
Witche's Altar 107
Characters on the first side of the athame 111
Characters on the second side of the athame 111
Characters on the bolline 113
Characters of the cup .115
Simple Pentacle 117
Golden Dawn Pentacle 117
Elaborate Pentacle. 118
Characters on the incense burner. 119
Characters appearing on the candleholders 122
Characters of the Book of Shadows 124
Traditional characters on the wand 128
Invoking and Banishing Pentagrams 152
The art of anointing candles with oils. 190
Lunar phases 250
The Wheel of the Year. 268
Familiar SPORASS, as illustrated by the author 306
Open Hexagram Layout 317
A divinatory spread 321

Language note

Although male practitioners may be referred to as *wizards* and female as *witches*, it is customary to use the term "witch" or "witches" to refer to both. In order not to burden the text unnecessarily, when *Witch* or *Witches* is used in this book (being a feminine noun), it is intended for practitioners of both genders.

PROLOGUE

SINCE the beginning of my magickal career, I have had many opportunities to see how Magick is a fascinating subject, for a very large majority of people. Even more, how Magick seemed to attract an ever-increasing number of new followers, and this, year after year. But above all, I also note with a stupefied eye how, by this very high demand for works dealing with esoterism, occultism, Magick and witchcraft, we have seen the birth of new authors who were still unknown to us to this day.

Having the opportunity to choose among different books on Magick is excellent. To be able to compare authors with each other in order to form our own opinion; to know who says true and who says false, that is even better. In this regard, my experience tells me just how much some books of Magick can, unfortunately, be so poor, so much from the point of view of their content than in terms of information. It seems, according to my own perspective, that many are improvising themselves authors only in the sole purpose of selling to carefree and profane people cheap books lacking in depth. I find this way of doing things totally deplorable because it is my humble opinion that an author, whoever he may be, has responsibilities towards his readers, and, consequently, that he must ensure that he provides an exemplary and accurately filled content, to the best of his ability and knowledge. Because after all, it is you, dear reader who will put this learning into practice and it is therefore essential that you can hold truthful and adequate information. Please be vigilant.

If you're wondering what are my motives to share these revelations with you, it is simply that as an author and experienced magician, I have too often seen naive people rely on lower-class books and unfortunately gobbling up everything that was written in them! That is why I decided to write this witchcraft formulary; so I may correct, somehow, a situation that seems to persist and to bring to esoteric literature a book that, I hope, will finally satisfy everyone's expectations, from novice practitioners to more advanced adepts.

Of course, I will never have the pretension to say that this very work you hold in your hands is far superior to all the others, no, it will be up to you to judge for yourself. But rather, that it was written with love and passion for Magick and with this intimate concern for accuracy and authenticity of the mass of information it contains. If this book succeeds to serve as a reference and make you discover new notions, and I am convinced that it will, if the latter can properly teach you the basic rudiments of witchcraft and that it can make you grow by applying the true precepts of natural White Magick, known today as Wicca, then my efforts will not have been in vain.

I sincerely hope that this witchcraft formulary will open your mind and expand your consciousness to whole new horizons, and that it will succeed in dusting off this lot of misunderstood knowledge since the human intellect became interested in the sciences of the invisible.

INTRODUCTION

H AVE you ever wondered what is witchcraft; how one truly became a witch; how these practitioners of the White Art practiced their charms and magickal rituals; where did they get their knowledge and how did they apply it in their daily lives?

If you answered yes to even one of these questions, then this book is especially for you. Because by reading this book of witchcraft, you will find all these answers and much more. Do you want to become a true witch? Then read this book carefully. It will teach you to practice Magick *effectively*.

Witches have populated our tales and legends since immemorial times. Too often wrongly accused and singled out in the past, because their knowledge far exceeded the understanding of an unconscious public mass of the different levels of existence, these beings, often working in hiding and surrounded by an aura of mystery, have always, after all, fascinated us quite a bit.

Witchcraft, which is an Art as old as the Earth, was long handed down from generations to generations, from adepts to adepts, from witches to witches. A tradition whose deep roots have survived the erosion of time, the initiatory teachings of the past has largely contributed into training the witches, herbalists, clairvoyants, astrologers and occultists of today. As far back as we can go in history, we find inevitable traces of Magick in every continent and within all cultures.

Now, here we are at a time where knowledge is more than ever within reach, but we still need to know where to turn to obtain these pieces of wisdom and scholarship in order to admit them into our lives. Some will see it as an opportunity to become charlatans, while on the contrary, a handful of righteous conscious people will seize the moment to push the false prophets of yesterday so that the true knowledge of the Universal energies can be part of tomorrow.

With the coming of the Aquarius era, many things fortunately began to change. Information suddenly became much more accessible to us; people seem, in part, to become more open-minded and ready to accept new truths, as old as they may be! New adepts and practitioners show themselves more easily in its true light, while others will continue to practice under the seal of secrecy and anonymity. The veil cloaking Magick has gradually begun to dissipate.

With this new edition published for the first time in English, I'm happy to finally reach out to the rest of you who could not find suitable to follow the true teachings of Witchcraft with a book previously available only in my mother's tongue. The situation has now been addressed. It is my humble hope that this manual will be welcomed as a new tool to perfect your learnings in the Pagan and Magickal Arts.

One thing remains certain; the Gods, the Old Ones, will always and more than ever be solicited and in demand...

M-A Ricard ~ 555

FIRST PART

The Awakening of the Witch

PURE & SIMPLE MAGICK

Magick is a pure and unique science. Magick is ONE.

WITCHCRAFT is a popular form of Magick practiced by witches. We often refer to this Art in more simplified terms, Wicca, which is a magickal philosophy of life in respect of nature, or simply the practice of white Magick. But is white Magick the same as witchcraft? Yes, it is identical in a certain way. Any form of non-selfish or harmful Magick could be properly considered by "white Magick" or beneficial Magick. Unfortunately, we always tend to label anything around us in order to classify and group everything into various categories, for the sake of dividing what is good from what is bad, what is white from what is black.

Magick is a whole, and therefore, a unique science that possesses at the same time several disciplines or rather, I would say, many fields of expertise. In a pictorial way, imagine for a moment that if Magick was represented by a tree, we could say that witchcraft would correspond to one of its branches. However, witchcraft is not the ultimate magickal practice, it is rather a part of the whole that is Magick. From another angle, if Magick was perceived as an orchestra, witchcraft could be the group of strings, violins and cellos, High Magick would be the brass while Ceremonial Magick would correspond to the percussions and so on. What is important to remember, dear reader, is that Magick embraces all occult and hermetic sciences and all esoteric traditions. Magick is the Science of sciences; it is ONE.

Furthermore, you should know that Magick does not have a "color" per see, it is neither white nor black. I was able to see with some amusement how many people label the various practical aspects of magickal science. Over time, we have come to obtain white magick, black magick, red magick, green... and so on! But then, are there so many types of Magick? No. Once again, Magick is a unique science, it is a set of practices and beliefs, of spiritual Laws and philosophies of life; it is several paths connected to the same center, several rays going in different directions, but all connected to the same central sun.

Associating a specific color with a magickal discipline comes from the fact that most practitioners express themselves in simplified terms. For example, for many, red is symbolic of love and, therefore, "red magick" was born to designate magickal practices having a direct relationship with love and sentimental life. To make sure you can fully grasp the meaning of my words, I will quote you a very acceptable definition of Magick:

> *Magick is the Art and Science of making changes in accordance with will, applying the Universal and Natural Laws, for the good of oneself or others, consciously or unconsciously.*

Based on this last definition, we can easily understand that everything depends entirely on willpower. Thus, it is precisely the latter that will indicate the pseudo color of a magickal act. If this will is oriented towards the good and the Light, we could define a magickal act by White Magick. In contrast, if the will is focused on evil, darkness and wrong deeds, we could simplify our definition by Black Magick.

Thus, it is possible for you to simplify an aspect of magickal science as long as you can recognize that everything is based on the will and that a witch will always apply the same Laws for any cause, whether it concerns love, health, spirituality, etc. The same Universal Laws apply to that what is above as for what is below. There are no exceptions to this rule.

Taking for granted that you have assimilated these important indications and to make the reading of this book easier, I will therefore opt from now on for the terms of Witchcraft or White Magick.

That being said, a veil seems to constantly obscure some other important concepts of White Magick and these remain to be clarified so that you may be able to untangle this whole cluster of popular beliefs that tarnish the true identity of witchcraft. Life dictates to me that it is always my duty to inform you correctly to the best of my knowledge and it is on this path that I will therefore continue.

Witchcraft has no pejorative connotations and it rhymes in no way with darkness or black Magick. The reason why so many ignorant people believe that witchcraft is the science of evil is largely due to the psychological despotism imposed by the Catholic Church over the past few centuries. In those days, everything that could not be explained by men of the church, as much as it relates to the natural and occult sciences, simply became witchcraft... this famous trade with the devil! And that's how the stakes and witch hunts were born.

If one goes back in time, it is easy to notice how Christianity has attempted by all possible measures to suppress the movement of pagan practices. Among these acts of suppression, the erection of churches and holy places directly at the very sites where were commemorated formerly pagan celebrations and Sabbaths, sacred places to witches, skillfully chosen because of the vibratory quality produced by the nuclei of telluric forces, to name just this example.

Moreover, it will be obvious to you that several Catholic holidays fall, *by magic*, practically on the same dates as the Sabbaths still celebrated by witches at the present time. These last remarks will suffice to show how much witchcraft was, and still remains for many, totally despised.

Fortunately, witches are no longer tortured these days, but still, they are misunderstood in the eyes of a public mass, ignorant of life at another level. Yes, alas, people who do not fit with the daily grind (work, eat, sleep), will always be perceived differently from others. But this is also what sets you apart from the herd, you are unique and special beings and you are practicing a mysterious, enriching and such admirable discipline!

Practicing witchcraft will never mean casting evil spells against anything and everything that seems hostile to you. Remember that pure and simple Magick is a *NEUTRAL FORCE. Magick is the study and application of the Cosmic and Occult Laws of nature.* This science is therefore something entirely natural and it should even, in my humble opinion, be taught with the utmost respect for the benefit of each and every one.

Certainly, we do not live in a fairy tale where the world is joyful and life is seen through pink glasses. There will always be a counterpart to the good, an omnipresent duality. Again, as above so below...

That is why there will constantly be mean-spirited and malicious people attempting to appropriate and misuse these occult forces of nature for the sole purpose of satisfying various most questionable purposes. On the other hand, this should never, under any circumstances, tarnish the reputation of witchcraft because of a handful of angry and unconscious individuals.

At the risk of repeating myself, the witch who practices (or will eventually practice) Magick must from this moment recognize magickal power as a neutral force, raw and pure, which only asks to be modeled by one's own will. This power that will be in your hands could be compared to electricity. Electricity is a good example of brute force. If handled improperly, you risk causing very serious harm and electrocute yourself. On the other hand, if you know how to use it and properly channel its power, you will be able to operate household appliances or provide lighting for an entire city. Do you understand what I am getting at?

Always do good and your witchcraft practices will bring you the fruits of your hard work. You will even be able to fulfill some of your most cherished dreams. On the other hand, try even once to do evil, lose control of the energies and you risk getting sparks! Magick is pure, Magick can be simple, but the witch you will become must know how to be conscious and responsible for his actions at all times.

DO WE HAVE TO BE INITIATED TO BECOME A WITCH?

MY experience over many years of practice tells me that too many people mistakenly believe that the Magickal Arts are reserved only for initiates and elected individuals possessing innate occult gifts and talents. Too often, I have been asked by practitioners to be, whether it is possible to practice White Magick without having been initiated beforehand by a master, an experienced witch or a witch coven.

Stop! Whether you need to be initiated by another practitioner to become a witch, my answer will always be the same, no, it is not necessary. To this day, I still wonder where people find such erroneous indications. I know very well that those who wonder about this simply want to start their new magickal career on the right foot, by doing the right things. But remember this, there is no point in complicating your life; trust your intuition and it will guide you. Stay tuned to your heart. It is true, the Wicca tradition of the past required that only a witch could initiate another. But since, many things have fortunately changed and this strict principle is no longer an immutable rule.

The practice of White Magick is above all a way of life, a unique way to see the Universe around us; it is a personal and spiritual journey. Now, knowing that the vast majority of witches today practice in solitary, how do you imagine that they were introduced to witchcraft? Well, yes, by themselves.

It is true that witches' coven all possesses degrees of initiation aimed at properly supervising the adepts throughout their learning within the group. This is also true in regard of all magickal and esoteric orders that exist around the world. In witchcraft, the Wicca tradition has three degrees of initiation. The first degree or rite of passage expresses above all that the profane first becomes a member of the group of which he is now a part, and that he has demonstrated to possess all the skills and necessary knowledge required by the coven. He then becomes a proper witch. When he is ready to move to a higher level, then he can pass the second initiatory rite and so on.

The second initiatory degree grants the title of High Priest or High Priestess. This step clearly demonstrates, of course, that the witch has made great progress along the path of witchcraft. Obviously, the practitioner of the second degree will still remain under the tutelage and presidency of the coven's High Priest and High Priestess. He or she will now be able to initiate other members to the second degree.

The third and final degree of initiation elevates the witch to the last possible rank to attain. The witch becomes perfectly autonomous and will answer directly to the gods and her own consciousness. It will be possible, at this level, to initiate in turn the other witches to the third degree or even, under the approval of the leaders, to leave the group so to form his own coven.

However, remember the words I wrote: *a personal and spiritual journey...* To follow the path of witchcraft is therefore above all an individual choice that only concerns you. No one can compel you and no one can force you in any way. You don't want to be part of a group of witches for the moment, you want to go your own way and practice in solitary? Then do it according to your intuition; there is no doctrine to follow, nor any prerequisites except a passion for Magick! Remember the Wiccan Rede: *An ye harm none, do what ye will.*

This brief explanation of the initiatory degrees of witches' covens should serve only as a guide. In a modern context, there is no need to be part of a group to practice witchcraft because the degrees of initiation serve only those who wish to follow meticulously the rudiments of the Wicca tradition. I offer you, further in this book, the *Witch's Solitary Initiation Ritual.* The latter will be more than enough to introduce you to witchcraft by yourself, without resorting to anyone. Of course, if you ever want to be part of such a coven, then why not. But in the meantime, enjoy the practice of White Magick alone and above all, try to find joy and pleasure in it!

When I was a beginner myself, I met a wise witch, whose words of wisdom have always been engraved in my memory: "*If it seems good to you, then it must be good*". That is, do what feels right and if you feel comfortable with your choices, then it has to be good for you.

You feel attracted to White Magick, then just simply walk the path and do your own experiments. Explore this fascinating, enchanting and mysterious world. So, you want to become a witch? Then study carefully the teachings contained in this book, put into practice the rudiments that I will reveal to you and simply say... *I am!*

A TRADITION IN HARMONY WITH NATURE

WITCHCRAFT or the "old religion" is based on the awareness of nature and the Elements that come from it. One could say that the epicenter of Wicca is Mother Earth, Gaïa, the Earth being the plateau on which the forces of the Universe, the Sun and the Moon rest and join. This ancient pagan tradition, therefore, venerates all aspects of the Earth and of nature, which constantly regenerates itself through the uninterrupted cycle of births, life and death, to be reborn again.

Mainly based on respect for the Earth and the environment, Wicca saw its admiration diminish over the centuries with the coming of new religions and, above all, because of Christianity. Like most esoteric traditions, Wicca is an art of living, that of coexisting in the purest harmony with the forces of nature and living Beings, from men to animals, from trees and vegetation to stones and minerals.

For the witch, everything that exists has its purpose and each thing has its own specific properties. Nothing is useless and everything that lives has the right to respect.

For your information, there are different branches or Wicca traditions. Like the Gardnerian and Alexandrian ones, each with its own rules of ethics and codes of conduct. But no matter the tradition, all are alike because they advocate the same ideologies and concepts in the face of the harmony of nature and Earth.

Furthermore, Wicca also uses a dualistic approach of life and the natural forces it respects. Indeed, this tradition recognizes as supreme power not a single divine source or a single god-of-all, but rather two well-defined identities (or Entities) personifying the Universal energies: the God and the Goddess, the Sun and the Moon. Witches have always relied on a double power, the God possessing all the attributes of the masculine current and the Goddess for her qualities representing the feminine principle. From this cosmogony were born, among others things, the solar and the lunar rites and those celebrating the passing of the seasons; the sabbatical feasts, related to the many beliefs as well as to the metaphorical mythology of the deities.

Witches will never say that their tradition (or religion) is superior to any other. Indeed, today it is possible to integrate the principles of witchcraft into your own religion, if your conscience allows it. Witches recognize the supreme power of the God and the Goddess whose essence is found in all creation and all things. But even more, they also recognize the existence of other gods and goddesses, of different pantheons of deities, and will never deprive themselves of appealing to them when needs require it.

In addition, it should be noted that the Wicca tradition is organized hierarchically, precept which is found practically within all magickal orders. At the head of each coven are a High Priest and a High Priestess, thus displaying a fair balance of opposing and complementary forces. Still, duality is once again expressed and omnipresent.

In summary, adhering to this tradition will make you a person aware of his environment, of the small and large Universe, of the microcosm and macrocosm, of life that animates everything, of the workings of the Universe in all its greatness. Your approach to nature will be more spiritual and harmonious, as one with all that surrounds you, all that lives and breathes, all that exists, both on the material and on the invisible and spiritual planes.

Open your eyes, your heart and your consciousness wide to a higher level, let Life flow through you and constantly have this thirst for knowledge and you will become a powerful witch who, no matter the trials, will become one in harmony with nature, the Cosmos and the Universe.

LOW MAGICK OR HIGH MAGICK?

I WOULD now like to clarify a point that I find important at this stage of the book, namely: witchcraft; is it low or high magick?

Given that my field of expertise in Magick is mainly oriented towards the practices of High Magick, including the Bardonian[1] and kabbalistic system as advocated by the Hermetic Order of the Golden Dawn, it was quite normal, if not to say it seemed obvious to me, to elevate the rudiments of witchcraft contained in this book of Magick. Because indeed, when we know the advanced magickal techniques in compliance with Universal Laws, it then becomes easy to apply them and perform low Magick. It goes without saying that this is as valid for you as it is for me.

In this manner, I do not wish to alienate some of you,

---

1   Name given to the teachings of Master Arion, Franz Bardon.

although it may surprise you, but I must inform you that witchcraft, in the Wiccan tradition, for at least what is mostly found today in books, is considered *low Magick*. This does not mean you will degrade yourself if you become a witch! On the contrary, it merely means you will rather work from the basic principles of the Universe, that is, to cause a just return to the primordial sources of the human being, namely nature in all its simplicity and magnificence. There is no harm in practicing low Magick, and what's more, in my entire magickal career, I could say a conscious and well-trained witch can be a much more formidable opponent than a clunky magician! Just be aware that witchcraft represents only one branch in the tree of Magick Science; it is only one aspect of the purest and most authentic true Magick.

I must also admit that I deplore rigorously, if not to say that I have a very deep aversion towards some improvised (and ignorant) authors who have so largely contributed to improperly instructing the pursuers of the Magickal Arts and all witches to be, by revealing to them only very simplified aspects of witchcraft and the Wicca tradition, stipulating to readers that this was the highest form of Magick that exists. It is therefore easy to see why a good number of witches, newly followers, can imagine that practicing Magick is nothing more than casting little spells to obtain power and overcome financial, romantic causes, etc.

The Magickal Art, as indicated by High Magick, is lived day by day, it is a very noble philosophy of magickal and spiritual life in accordance with the Universal forces. This is not something that we do from time to time or worse, only when something is out of our control. To become a witch is to become a High Priest, a High Priestess of the energies of nature and Cosmos.

Of course, ritual practice will soon become an integral part of your life. By reading this witchcraft formulary, you will soon discover how to transform your daily life by tuning in to the natural forces and interacting with those same energies for your own benefit and that of other people you cherish. But please, don't stop there. The Universe, Life and nature are so vast that they are worth taking the time to contemplate and question yourself. He who practices witchcraft will perform rituals and charms, of course, but the real witch will know there is something greater than simply casting spells. By now following the path of witchcraft, you will incessantly discover a thousand and one wonders.

On the other hand, if you have already read other available books on White Magick, it is quite possible that you may find this book differs from what you may have seen before. That this book, in comparison, has many more technical elements to carry out your subsequent magickal practices. In other words, if you feel at times that my explanations become complicated, it is most likely that you have always been told that Magick is easy to practice, within everyone's reach and that it requires no knowledge. Naturally, you will agree this is completely false. Anyone who does not want to put in the effort will never obtain anything in return. Enlighten your mind and study your Art, but even more, practice, practice and practice! This is the key to success.

Getting back to my words about low Magick, not only do I offer you in this book all the authentic fundamental precepts of witchcraft, but I also decided, to do things right, and teach you several notions of High Magick, which blends perfectly with witchcraft. They are, in my humble opinion, essential if not vital, to practice effectively your Art.

We could therefore say, rightly so, that this work is a true book of *High Witchcraft*.

THE WITCHES' REDE & FUNDAMENTAL PRINCIPLES

Ain't harm none, do what you will.

THAT'S it. Everything is there. This simple sentence sums up the witches' attitude perfectly. The witches' Rede beautifully expresses how you should behave when you use your magickal power and all your occult knowledge. Without ever and in no way wishing harm to anyone, without ever falling into the trap of black magick and never interfering in the life path of others without their consent, you possess what is called free will, and therefore, the intimate choice to accomplish everything you wish to do.

For witches, nothing is impossible. Any obstacle can be overcome with a little willpower and the required effort. However, the key to this Rede lies in how you will manifest your powerful magickal will. Do not forget, beware of the boomerang effect of your magick because you will always be held responsible for your acts in witchcraft... there is no escape! The following chapter will deal with karma and the Law of the Triple Return. Pay special attention to it because it is this Law that should dictate your conduct throughout your career as a witch.

In addition, even if the practice of White Magick is very permissive, allow me to emphasize that, despite if you have carte blanche to try all the magickal experiments of your choice, remember that you should never attempt to cause harm to others. A witch works only for constructive purposes, for good and light, never to destroy, nor for darkness and evil. You will find this last sentence in the fundamental principles. The reason I mention it here at this exact moment, is because of its utmost importance to remember.

However, the Rede is a phrase recognized by all witches that also demonstrates there is, strictly speaking, no strict code of conduct among practitioners of this Magick Art, apart from not harming anyone, directly or indirectly. Witchcraft is, therefore, a way of life that promotes free expression and freedom, as is also the nature to which this tradition is so intimately linked. That should enchant you right now. Because you are a future witch and you are already as free as a bird!

Aside from this interesting point, I believe it is now essential to share with you the fundamental principles of witchcraft so that you can be well mentored throughout your first solitary steps on the path of White Magick. Dear reader, perceive me now as a simple guide who opens the way and points you a suitable route.

Over the years, I have seen everywhere around me in discussions with witches that there seems to be laws in witchcraft, thirteen to be more precise. I do not want to be the bearer of bad news or worse, a prophet of doom, but I am in deep regret to inform you that these laws simply do not exist within this tradition. They are more than likely the fruit of a solitary author who decided to establish these few rules of conduct of his own and adapt them to witchcraft. I am not saying they are not valid, but simply that the Wicca tradition does not have these so-called laws. You see, each witch should instead have his/her own code of ethics based on his/her beliefs and life experiences, all in accordance with the Universal and Spiritual Laws that govern us all in this world. Everyone should then ideally be capable to forge their own rules based on good, justice and light.

True, when we are new to witchcraft, beginners or inexperienced, it is possible that we may have difficulty discovering, at the start of our magickal career, the guidelines that will influence and measure our White Magick behaviors, in a proper way. So, whether you are a novice witch or even more experienced, the following fundamental principles that I have developed for you will be of great assistance. Take the trouble to read them carefully and try to grasp all the meaning they convey.

These principles should ideally be followed and respected by all worthy witches, but if you believe that certain passages could be adapted according to your own convictions, then do so. Once again, allow me to point out that, as your guide teaching you witchcraft through this book, it implies I instruct you all the basics. I cannot, however, oblige you in any way. But after some repeated readings, you will undoubtedly notice that these foundations of witchcraft (and also the fruit of a solitary author) are all provided with accuracy and a very profound meaning, of that I am absolutely convinced.

The 20 Fundamental Principles of Witchcraft

I — Honor the God and the Goddess.

II — Honor Life for its splendor and perfection.
III — Honor nature for its splendor and perfection.

IV — Honor Mother Earth who has been lent to you as a living Being equal to yourself and respect Mother Earth, she who bears you within her womb.

V — Know yourself and recognize your limitations and abilities. Introspection opens the way to knowledge and wisdom.

VI — Admitting ignorance signifies the beginning of knowledge. Enlighten your intellect in this sense by studying the laws of Nature, Universal and Cosmic.

VII — Apply your knowledge with wisdom and discernment and practice your Art with awareness.

VIII — Work only for constructive purposes, for good and light, never to destroy, nor for darkness and evil.

IX — Direct your words and thoughts towards good, and cast away your negative words and reasonings from your mouth and mind. Words are creative. Thoughts are creative. Speak and think good and you will create goodness, speak and think evil and you will create evil.

X — Do not divulge your wisdom and knowledge to those who are not ready to hear it, for to do so would be pronouncing false truths.

XI — Never practice witchcraft in order to intervene on the life path of others without prior consent. Every living being must experience the trials that Life has laid before him.

XII — Seek balance by following the example of nature and harmonize with it and its life cycles.

XIII — Elevate yourself spiritually and accept reincarnation as a cycle allowing you to no longer commit mistakes now belonging to the past.

XIV — Meditate and learn to listen in the silence of your heart. Connect yourself to the Cosmic Light and Universal energies, and allow them to flow through you.

XV — Respect Creation and all living creatures, large or small. They are all equal to each other and all have their reason of being. All deserve your recognition.

XVI — Recognize the different planes of existence and the various zones of density. These places are inhabited, just like your world on a higher or other level of consciousness than yours. Life exists beyond the perception of your eyes.

XVII — Ask the help of Entities and Higher Spheres, invoke them often. If you demand nothing, you will receive nothing.

XVIII — Master your own personal Universe if you aspire one day to master the Universe in which you interact.

XIX — Recognize the Law of Karma and of Triple Return and thus you will know that if you sow good you will reap good. If you sow evil, you will reap evil. Everything will be handed back to you one day or another, in this life or another.

XX — Without harming none, do what you will.

KARMA: LAW OF INCARNATIONS & TRIPLE RETURN

Who sows the wind shall reap whirlwind,
who sows flowers will reap roses.

As seen earlier, the 19th fundamental principle of witchcraft dictates the following: *Recognize the Law of Karma and of Triple Return and thus you will know that if you sow good you will reap good. If you sow evil, you will reap evil. Everything will be handed back to you one day or another, in this life or another.*

In order to understand and interpret the law of karma, but above all, to make sure you can become aware of its impact in your everyday life as well as during your magickal practices, some explanations are most necessary.

Everyone has heard of karma at least once in their lives, if only humorously: "Oh! This person is so unlucky, it's incredible, it must be bad karma." But what exactly is karma? To begin with, karma is a Universal Law very intimately linked to the cycles of incarnations. To fully integrate this concept of life, know that you must undoubtedly believe in reincarnation and renewed life cycles. Otherwise, the law of Triple Return will have no impact nor visible effect on your consciousness, but of course, you will still be subject to it, without realizing it. Remember; *it is not because we are unaware of the existence of a Law, that this one is not effective...*

To use simplified terms, making sure you can clearly understand me, imagine karma as a cosmic matrix that records all your deeds and gestures, all your thoughts and words, in short, all your behaviors. Every action you pursue will therefore be recorded there. But even more, know that each of your actions will reverberate all around you and will influence all that surrounds you, both within human beings as from a purely energetic point of view.

Karma serves primarily for the spiritual evolution of every individual living on the planet; our dear Mother Earth. Why do I say this law is for spiritual evolution? Know that the first goal of every human being should ideally be getting closer to perfection, learn from the mistakes of the past and not reproduce them in the future and finally to pursue this path of spiritual evolution consciously rising to a higher level of existence.

The 19th principle of witchcraft also informs us that *everything will be handed back to you one day or another, in this life or another.* This is one of the reasons why karma can also be considered a law of causes and effects. The experiences and sufferings you endure in this present life are also due to your karma. The bad choices you have made and the bad actions of your past (both in this life and previous lives) brings you struggles and situations today where you will once again be facing the same choices of yesteryear. If you cannot overcome these trials and therefore, at the same time, purify your karma, you will once more have to come back in a future incarnation in order to have the opportunity to make the right choice when the time comes again.

And so goes life. You have trials to overcome, trials which have been assigned to you by your own actions (and which you have agreed to live through) before incarnating this physical body on the earthly plane. They are like tests you have to pass to rise spiritually in order to move on. These struggles, that life sends you are due to your karma. To help you grasp these complex notions, imagine the following:

You are a psychic and possess this ease for clairvoyance. Very quickly your reputation outstrips you wherever you go and everyone rushes to meet you for advice. People confide in you and in your ability to see the future, and those who seek consultation expect you to be able to give them the best way forward to help them get out of the most diverse situations. Seeing you have a very strong influence on the people you meet, you decide one day to employ this force to make people do what you like and to deceive them for your one and only profit. You manage to extract money from everyone and your dishonest life ends on this note. Then you incarnate again, and because of your karma, this time you experience a life of misery. You are despised by everyone you encounter; you are a poor and harmless beggar that everyone laughs at.

What should you make out of this little story? Try by yourself and when you think you have found the reason, read on. Our medium has, throughout his dishonest life, taken advantage of the blind trust and naivety of his entourage in order to earn a lot of money telling false truths. This fictional person took advantage of his great influence to deceive others. These acts have been recorded and as everything we do will be handed to us one day or the other, in this life as in another, our medium finds himself now living an existence of distress in which all despise him. He reaped the fruits of his past seeds and today he suffers terribly. Was Life unfair to him? Not at all, she made him taste his own medicine and today, without being aware of it, he will have to endure these trials to purify his heavy karma. Our medium had the confidence of his entourage while today everything is to be rebuilt.

Obviously, this story could have had a completely different conclusion. Our fictional psychic could just as easily have found himself in the same incarnation cycle with similar talents of clairvoyance, in a practically identical situation. Then again, despite acknowledging his past mistakes, even by being ardently determined to make amends, to redeem himself and to honestly help others, perhaps he would have found it difficult to get paid by his clients, and even worse, he would have had no clientele for his services and much trouble being recognized for his talent. One way or the other, Life will take care of the rest of the events.

That being said, your karma can thus increase by accumulating karmic debts or gradually lighten up according to the choices you will make throughout your life. It is up to you and you alone to make the right choices for your greater good, not only as a witch, but also as a Being of a spiritual nature. The secret to circumventing karma is however so simple; always lead a healthy life, direct your witchcraft practices towards noble goals and you will hardly have that sword of Damocles hovering over your head.

As a result, the Law of Karma also known as the Law of the Triple Return stipulates what you bring into this life will reverberate three times on your daily life and what you experience will be in perfect analogy to your own actions and thoughts. In other words, practice harmful witchcraft, surrender to black magick and you will reap trouble threefold. In contrast, do good in your White Magick rituals and around you, and it will return to you thrice.

HOW TO EFFECTIVELY FORMULATE REQUESTS DURING RITUALS

I T is funny how some people react to the Law of Karma. Indeed, some practitioners who deliberately try to cross the thin line between beneficial and harmful witchcraft say they recognize the effectiveness of their negative magick in the sense that, shortly after performing a ritual, an uninterrupted chain of bad luck follows, results generated by the boomerang effect of the Triple Return. It goes without saying that witches who act this way are completely unconscious and that this attitude should be very severely proscribed.

Consequently, in order to make you avoid the missteps during the beginning of magickal career, I will explain how you will need to formulate your requests during ritual practices so that you cannot go into karmic debt, nor commit serious faults that you may later have to pay at a very high price.

The principle of causing harm to others through an act of witchcraft can be defined in terms of physical, moral, psychological or psychic harm. Aside from karmic repercussions, witches possess a deep knowledge of Universal Laws. They recognize that everything in the Universe is interconnected. All things are linked to each other. As a consequence, the witches know that any act taken will affect their environment and therefore, if we recognize this principle, any action must necessarily be directed towards the good of all. A magickal action will necessarily cause a powerful energy, a shock wave that will affect everything in its path.

It is in this perspective that witches who will practice rituals and spellcraft will need to know how to formulate their requests so their rituals can always end up symbolizing a magickal action that would result by the following sentence: "I wish to obtain this or modify that, as long as these changes happen without ever causing harm to anyone." The responsible witch, who knows how to answer for her actions and who will work by this rule, will always work wisely, because to act otherwise would be to become an agent of chaos.

For this purpose, it turns out sometimes that even with the best intentions in the world, you would end up practicing, without your knowledge, a form of black Magick. A magick that could act and interfere with the life path of someone and corrupt his free will. Remember, a witch can easily practice Magick for her own good, to drastically change her life and improve it, but under no circumstances should the effects produced by rituals coerce a person or harm him in any way whatsoever. In this regard, I will explain to you later how to effectively practice divination in order to see the possible outcomes of your witchcraft and prevent such situations.

The best example I can give you to illustrate everything I have just explained, is that of love charms. A majority of people think that love is a good thing; it makes us happy, expressive, love makes us go crazy in its name, in short, love rhymes with bliss. Those who practice witchcraft realize it will be very easy for them, thanks to certain magickal skills, to cast love spells in order to live this coveted happiness. And here is where inexperienced witches quickly fall into the trap.

The witch who manipulates a third party and forces him to fall in love, automatically means depriving him of his most sacred right, his own free will. To demand through a magickal ritual that a person loves you is to be insensitive to the feelings of other, it is exactly as if you say, 'I don't care if you don't love me, because from now on, thanks to my magickal powers, you will!'

Do witches act this way? Yes, unfortunately too often! Of course, I was saying the mistake was in the witch's unconscious state of mind. For if in your eyes, love is an honorable feeling, how could it harm anyone... love is so beautiful! Indeed, that seems very fair. Most of you have already or will make this mistake sooner or later, and that is why I had to warn you at this time. Too often, I have found that love magick is one of the strongest reasons why people turn to witchcraft. These people are experiencing emotional deprivations and no longer know how to attract this love that will overwhelm them. They hear about spellcrafting and the possibilities to obtain love through magick, and the rest is history...

As I mentioned earlier, the ideal method for not forcing anyone's free will through magickal practices is how you formulate requests during rituals. You will always be able to get everything your heart desires, but you will have to be careful how you ask for it. A witch is free to influence and manipulate the energies of nature in order to accomplish a very specific goal, however, she has no right to manipulate people. Witches believe in justice, not revenge. They know that what must happen will inevitably occur.

If you are wondering at this moment whether it is possible to get love properly through witchcraft without harming anyone, my answer is affirmative; yes, this is more than feasible. You can always circumvent manipulation situations by acting directly on your own hindrances. For example, instead of asking for a specific individual to love you, during a ritual, rather ask that all the obstacles that obstruct the passage of love in your life be removed from you or that the right person for you to come to you. Perhaps the effect of the ritual will ensure that someone who secretly loves you will be able to overcome shyness and finally decide to take the first steps! In the end you will gain love, but you will get it the right way, without harming others.

As there is never better than sharing personal experiences to understand and learn, I will provide you a second example; how once I have myself respected this law of free will and how I performed a ritual by preventing a situation that would have immediately induced me to practice black magick against an unknown rival.

Many years ago, while I was still in the stage of magickal learning (and likely will always be, so much there is to learn) there was a friend I was dating. We were in love with each other, and everything was well. But then came a day when my beloved informed me that a certain man was hovering around her and flirting with her. Initially, it did not affect me because I had confidence in myself and trusted my girlfriend. Unfortunately, although she took the trouble to tell the man in question she was already in a relationship and she no longer wanted to be bothered by his advances, he persisted rigorously and pursued his little game. After two or three weeks, seeing according to my girlfriend's words that the situation was beginning to escalate, becoming much more complex than I would have imagined, and that she no longer knew how to avoid this young man who was causing her so much trouble and discomfort, I decided to take drastic measures and remotely take action, thanks to my knowledge of witchcraft.

The first thought that came to my mind was that, if he was sick, stuck in bed, he would have to stay home to treat himself and would no longer bother my girlfriend. Of course, it was a completely stupid idea that I immediately drove out of my mind. I did not want to wish anyone harm and so I had to find an alternative. Finally, on a sunny afternoon, I practiced a ritual. The purpose of the ritual was simply that this person, whose name I was able to obtain, could meet the right person and find the love that suited him. Later, after about a week, my girlfriend told me that she had once more encountered the young man and that he had not even paid attention to her as usual, because he and another woman were kissing passionately and seemed to be most in love!

Thus, while respecting the free will of my rival, I achieved my ends without causing harm to anyone. He found the ideal person for him and realized my girlfriend was not the right one to receive his love. The situation was quickly resolved without stirring waves. You see, anything is possible. Just think a little and find out how to formulate your requests during rituals for the greater good of all.

In summary, this rule must be applied to all the requests you make during occult work of witchcraft. Understand that the God and the Goddess watch over you from this very moment; they know how to read your heart and they see your intentions and weaknesses. Inevitably, they will be able to answer your calls if you know how to formulate them correctly with consciousness.

ACQUIRING WITCHES' MAGICKAL POWERS

SINCE you are now a witch, you must promptly pay careful attention to this present chapter. It will deal with the fundamental magickal powers related to the practice of witchcraft. These powers, which I will explain how to develop and maintain, are six in number. They will represent the six basic pillars on which all your magickal actions will be based, namely:

- ☆ Will
- ☆ Visualization
- ☆ Intuition
- ☆ Faith
- ☆ Meditation
- ☆ The sense of the mystery

Practicing witchcraft can be extremely effective. But to

achieve the most complete success possible, you will need to exercise your new powers in order to become fully operational when you want to move on to the practical side of White Magick, that is, to practice rituals of magick and ceremonies.

Although Wiccan witches frequently use accessories of all kinds in their occult practices, true witches recognize that Magick is first and foremost within them and that everything operates from that personal power that everyone possesses. However, in witchcraft, you will frequently have to employ various auxiliaries and accessories. But remember; the magickal power does not lie in these artifices, although they may possess many occult properties. No, this creative force of manifestation, **this real magickal power is IN YOU and nowhere else**. Tap into your resources and you will be able to accomplish whatever your heart desires.

Right now, these powers, these talents, lie dormant in each of you. They are concealed deep within your psyche. With a little training, you will be capable to awaken them so they later become second nature to you. If in the past you have tried to practice witchcraft without success, perhaps you were missing this little something essential: a basic witches' training. You want your magickal practices to be successful, don't you? So, train seriously and I promise you will achieve the success you deserve.

✶ **Will** ✶

The first power to exercise is the will. It goes without saying that the development of a strong will is one of the main goals of practitioners of the White Art. The engine that feeds the magickal stream is the will, that intense force of desire. Willpower means wanting, and without that firm conviction of success, your magick can never exist.

During magickal operations, your will must never falter at any time; it is the force that will carry the fiery ardor of all your emotions and deep desires for something specific to happen, but most importantly, to come true. The foundation of all the magickal actions you will perform in White Magick will rest on this attitude that nothing can stand in your way. Your will must always be at the root of everything. If you don't want it hard enough, you definitely won't get it. A popular maxim states that when there's a will there's a way. Indeed, because if you *want*, you *can*.

To sharpen your willpower, you can resort to simple exercises that will be designed to develop your concentration. These will be very effective to help you forge a powerful and flawless sense of desire that nothing can compromise or impede. Among these exercises there are, of course, oriental disciplines such as yoga. But if you are unfamiliar with this type of exercise, do not worry, I will provide you tools that all witches frequently use to develop and tone this power with ease.

The first exercise consists in gazing a candle flame in calm and silence. Light a candle and sit comfortably. Stand about one or two meters from it. Then stare at the sparkling flame carefully and don't think about anything; clear your mind. Focus on seeing only this flame for about thirty minutes. Repeat this exercise as often as possible.

The second technique is very similar. However, instead of using a candle, take a white paper sheet and draw a perfect circle with black ink. Finally, make a point in the center of the circle. Now, stick your sheet on one of the walls of your workplace and sit in front. Stare carefully at the dot in the center of the circle without flinching, for about thirty minutes.

These two simplistic but very effective techniques will help you forge and maintain a strong willpower. In a short period of time, you will see how much your power will have increased significantly.

Following this, you can also, during your daily life, train yourself to submit your will on different subjects of experimentation. To begin with, practice on trivialities; there is no point in trying to accomplish unrealistic feats. Let it to the initiates to move the flame of a candle by simple mental action. Instead, try to subdue your power over small things that can be accomplished. For example, if you are walking around town, on a sidewalk, try getting the person in front of you to move aside to let you through. Same thing if you are in a car. Try to get the driver in front of you switch lanes and give you the way. These are just small, harmless examples; there are many more. Remember, however, not to try to manipulate people against their free will.

If you maintain this ambition to become a powerful white practitioner, without taking yourself for a god, try to cultivate your magickal will and strive to narrow the field of your attention to one and only thing. Therefore, try submitting your will to anything that can be. You may be very surprised by the results.

✰ **Visualization** ✰

Visualization is undoubtedly one of the greatest creative forces that exists. This second power will allow you to set in motion all the rituals that you will practice in the years to come. Consider visualization your weapon of choice for all your magickal operations.

Being able to visually represent the purpose of a specific magickal action, as if it had already been realized, will allow you to sustain your power of thought. Knowing from the outset that, as with visualization, thought is also creative on another plane of existence and that any firmly renewed and sustained thought will sooner or later manifest itself on the physical plane, if the latter is supported by a strong mental imagery, the power of thought will automatically be multiplied tenfold as well as your chances of success during your rituals.

Visualization is also synonymous with imagination. The more the roots of your visions plunge into your sensibilities and the stronger they become, the more powerful your mental imagery will be to concretize your rituals and charms. When you find yourself inside your magick circle, sometimes expect to have to grind your teeth, pursue fast dances, gesticulate in all directions, or even go into trance. In essence, all these gestures could help to support your power of visualization and imagination in order to excite your visions and trigger the current initiator of your practices of witchcraft.

Be aware that visualization is used in almost all magickal practices. Without it, little can be achieved and that is why you will need to exercise this power to the best of your ability, with determination. Combining thought and visualization will make you a powerful practitioner of the Art. All your hope of success through witchcraft will depend, among other things, on this essential faculty.

To effectively be able to develop your power of visualization through which all your mental images will be realized, practice the following exercise as often as possible, until you can master it without any difficulty.

Sit comfortably and close your eyes. Picture in your mind an ordinary and simple object to begin with, such as a spoon, a pencil or even a match. In short, find a visualization topic and represent it as clearly as possible in your mind. Maintain this mental image for at least ten minutes without flinching. Try seeing the chosen object as if it were truly and physically in front of you. Contemplate it in all its fine details. Observe it thus in the same way as if it was with your eyes of flesh. If various thoughts or other images were to disturb the course of this exercise, immediately drive them away and push them forcefully, then continue your concentration work.

It is possible at first, especially for people who have never practiced visualization, that you may have difficulty maintaining a clear and sharp image for a long period of time or even a few seconds. Do not worry if that is the case. Redouble your efforts and continue this exercise with firmness and the conviction that you can do it. When you are successful, repeat the same exercise, but this time keeping your eyes open. Once you are capable to visualize an object of your choice, you will see how easy it will to later imagine complete and elaborate scenes.

✮ **Intuition** ✮

For some people, intuition may seem like a meaningless concept without much importance or utility. However, witches recognize intuition as a truly powerful force that does indeed possess its *raison d'être* among the six fundamental pillars of witchcraft.

You all know roughly, in your own words, what intuition is. This little inner voice, that seems to show you from time to time the path to follow and the actions you should perhaps take. This simple definition is accurate, but this power is slightly more complex than that. It is therefore up to me to explain it to you as clearly as possible.

Too frequently I was told that we had all the answers hidden deep within ourselves; that we do not have to seek the truth elsewhere, because without being aware of it, we carried it deep in our soul. But more often still, I could see how this was of the greatest truths. He who knows how to listen to his inner self, will discover a being imbued with wisdom who only asks to provide right advice.

In addition, the notions of intuition can be from the simplest to the most complicated explanations. First, know that you are a Divine Being and that if that Being is directly connected to nature and the Universe and lets the Cosmic energies flow through him, as indicated by the 14th fundamental principle of witchcraft, as are all witches, then you possess a very great advantage, a precious power that is your own.

If you are able to connect directly to Life and Mother Earth, they will communicate a thousand and one things to you; various essential informations that only you will be capable to understand and interpret for your unique evolution and well-being.

That said, there are unfortunately too frequently practitioners who nowadays work only through books, without questioning themselves in any way and lacking relying on their own judgment, thus strictly following the manuals and recipes never derogating from them. On the other hand, some will rather see magick rituals as a kind of basis from which, and according to their awareness of the moment, they can implement their own personal modifications by following their instincts. And the witch's instinct is obviously called... intuition!

So how does intuition work? First of all, there is your subconscious that is constantly trying to send you messages. These messages, ranging from simple images to strange and mysterious concepts, are often difficult to decipher. They occur most of the time when you are asleep and dreaming. And that is why we often say *"I'll sleep on it"*, because it is exactly the most favorable time for your subconscious to communicate to you some relevant information. When you are asleep, your consciousness withdraws and you become very receptive.

Second, many practitioners are able to receive messages from the Higher Spheres of consciousness, that is, suggestions that come directly from Entities and Beings inhabiting subtle planes. Some benevolent Entities will try influencing you for your own good, much like a personal guide. However, you will also need to be wary of malicious Beings trying to influence you for the sole purpose of misleading you or seeing you perform acts for their sole benefit. Caution and discernment are therefore in order.

Finally, I could also tell you that it is possible that, from incarnations to incarnations, the consciousness of a Being can sometimes experience the phenomenon of *instant recall*. It merely means that, without knowing the reason, you suddenly feel you know an undeniable truth without being able to explain how you have this feeling of accuracy. This phenomenon can be explained as follows. Throughout your incarnations, you have amassed an impressive wealth of knowledge and diverse experiences. Now it is more than possible that a specific trigger brought you to *remember*, as if a flash of comprehension had instantly illuminated your consciousness with a long-forgotten knowledge belonging to a very distant past, going back to a previous life.

From a practical point of view in magick, it is very likely that one day you will experience a certain impulse guiding you towards some act, even occurring in the middle of a ritual. Then you could interpret this message as a path to follow. In due course, whether you should give it free rein, will only depend solely on your judgment.

As you have just seen, it is impressive to recognize how intuition can be the result of many various factors. Either way, no matter how you get revelations or ideas, always try to rely on your instinct. Normally, intuitions are always good omens and should be listened to.

☆ Faith ☆

The fourth power of witches is based on faith. All the strength conveyed during the rituals and all the magickal power that you can show will depend largely on it. It doesn't matter whether you indulge in a simple incantation or a more complex ceremony. An unwavering faith that nothing or no external power can affect is essential.

If will is synonymous with wanting, faith itself undoubtedly means believing. Remember this: through faith, the imagination is strengthened, for any doubt will harm its realization. I can't tell you enough that believing in your abilities is more than important; it is vital. If you can't have trust your in your sorcery, then who can?

In addition, you will find that faith is intrinsically linked to visualization, imagination and will. Because to be capable to represent a specific goal in a ritual in order to achieve it, you will first have to be able to picture it mentally. To be able to do this, you also need to wish for this thing happen, and to want a ritual to be effective, you must first believe in it, with all your might; believe in yourself and your magick; but even more, believe beyond any doubt your desire will come true. Some mote it be.

If you cannot have absolute faith in your own magickal powers, you will never reach the required state of consciousness and the desired intensity to practice witchcraft effectively. In the same vein, if you perform a magickal ritual just to see if it works, then you are questioning its effectiveness, and obviously it won't work. One of the greatest obstructions to magickal success is doubt, because to doubt is to fail. Burn these words in your memory, today and forever.

By casting doubt out of your mind, believing you deserve what you desire to obtain through magickal practices and showing unwavering faith, you will then be able to sweep away all the pitfalls that would be inclined to impede success. You will then be capable to build in yourself a moment of faith and cultivate this state of mind. Your faith, combined with your other magickal powers and skills, will prepare the way to greatness, the secret of success in all true actions in the practice of witchcraft. It is stated that faith can move mountains, just think about it...

☆ **Meditation** ☆

Meditation is a technique that everyone knows. But do you know exactly what comes of it to practice such an exercise? It is not a matter of merely sitting in the lotus position, index fingers against thumbs verbalizing *aum*. Admittedly, for some people, this is pretty much in line with their way of doing things. Of course, there must be as many ways of meditating as there are schools of thought.

For my part, I will teach you a simple and very effective method of which results you will soon be able to observe with a minimum of serious practice.

Meditation is the process by which a practitioner can enter a state of receptive passivity. It is also one of the methods *par excellence* to connect to the Universal and nature energies in order to allow them flow into you. The dividends you can expect from meditation are as follows: you will be able to connect to the Universal energies by opening yourself wide to them. Furthermore, by connecting into these energies in passiveness, without forcing your mind, which will stay at the neutral point, you will be able to receive information or obtain visions of any kind. I personally know some people who get a lot of amazing information when they enter a meditative semi-trance state.

Other benefits may also be expected. Note, for example, that a practitioner of the Art who meditates frequently will become much more powerful. Indeed, by controlling his mind this way, he will never be distracted when he engages in ritual practice. His mind will be fully aligned and focused where it belongs and nowhere else. Meditation will therefore, at the same time, strengthen his capacity for concentration and the power of his will.

Dear witch, just know that meditating regularly will bring you a state of bliss. You will be able to escape yourself from your daily life and what is more, you will also be able to get in touch with the forces belonging to higher Spheres, even directly with the God and the Goddess.

Among all the techniques of meditation, there is one I particularly like, and without further delay, I will introduce you to it. True meditation consists in being able to tame one's mind to such an extent that no thought can form itself in our mind; there must reign the most complete emptiness. At first glance, you might tend to say it is easy to think of nothing, but in fact, it is a relatively difficult exercise to master, especially if you are a beginner in this field.

If desired, stand behind your altar and light one to three candles. Burn a quality incense such as rose or frankincense. I invite you to refer to the chapter dealing with incense and plant compositions to find which one you could use to obtain the most beneficial effects to adjust the vibratory rate.

Now take a comfortable position so that you can forget about your physical body for the duration of this exercise and close your eyes. Relax and try to empty your entire mind and chase away any thoughts or mental images you might have. Focus on the darkness, that feeling of emptiness and silence. Open your heart and mind to the Higher Spheres; connect with the magnificence of the Universe. Then stay in this state as long as possible. This is the basic technique of meditation. Use it as often as you can.

Obviously, you're a witch, and so your possibilities do not end there. If you wish to use meditation to achieve a much more precise effect, like receiving answers to a given subject, when you are centered, in the moment of opening your heart and mind, focus on the topic or question of your choice for a few minutes and then just let it go. You can simply set the tone for your meditation and then let the course of events follow on its own. If you put some commitment and seriousness into it, you will soon get the results you want to achieve.

☆ **The Sense of Mystery : Silence** ☆

The last pillar of witchcraft, and not the least, is the sense of mystery that can also be interpreted by silence or even secrecy. Knowledge is synonymous with power. When we know what are the foundations of a particular thing, in a given field of expertise, then we immediately hold a certain power over it. However, if knowledge is equivalent with power, sharing to others about one's actions in Magick, means losing power.

There are many reasons why you should always keep your magickal actions under the seal of secrecy and act rather clandestinely. Not that practicing witchcraft is wrong, quite the contrary! But in light of what will follow, you will easily understand my point of view on this matter.

The first reason, as I have just mentioned, is that if you inform those around you about your magickal practices, they will risk losing their effects or at most, they will be compromised and diminished. If someone learns you are going to conduct a ritual for a specific cause, the idea (the energy on the mental plane) that triggered this desire to perform the ritual in question will begin to spread and scatter all around you in the minds of the people you have spoken to about it. At this exact moment, the power of your acts of sorcery will come to be squandered unnecessarily. The energy that is preparing to manifest itself on the physical plane will have been absorbed by all who know. What will be the result? If anyone, even a very close friend of yours who you trust (but who does not share your beliefs) becomes aware that you are about to take action, it may, alas, be too late.

You must also consider the action of thought. Thought, as you know, can be creative as well as destructive. Thinking is, therefore, from the magickal point of view, a form of energy that can produce results that will eventually manifest. Thus, if one or more people know your actions, if they decide to get involved, even by simply thinking, *"He will not succeed, his magick will not work."* Such a thought targeted directly against you, even if the latter may seem innocuous, will cause an opposite effect that will echo in the Universe and will undoubtedly jeopardize your chances of success.

Creating a magick ritual requires a certain amount of energy and immediately sets in motion the mechanism of the creative power of thinking, because after all, deciding to move on to the practical side of witchcraft, it all began with an idea, a desire, a thought. Then comes the time to move on to the magick act itself. The ritual will deploy a strong dose of occult energies that will be directed towards the ultimate goal of the ritual. Then, these energies set in motion by your magick will eventually come to manifestation. If in the course of a magickal action a person were to create, even without his knowledge, contrary thoughts to your desire, and therefore, harmful energies that would momentarily block or slow down the free passage of your magickal power, your ritual may not trigger all the desired effects; the impact of your sorcery will be weakened. To this end, it is all about energy. The flood of energies deployed by a Magick ritual would risk losing its effectiveness if it encounters opposite energies along the way.

Of course, you still have the right to discuss about your magickal actions if you believe that the people you will entrust the secret to are trustworthy and will not put obstacles in your way. I can only recommend prudence. It will be up to you whether you want to put all the odds on your side or not. Besides, witches often say that after practicing a ritual, it is better to stop cogitating about it and let it act on its own. My last recommendation would therefore be to wait until you get the result of your practice of witchcraft before thinking speaking about it. Once the action is obtained, it will be safer to share it.

The 10th fundamental principle of witchcraft also offers you another good reason to keep the mystery about your actions. This principle says: *Do not divulge your wisdom and knowledge to those who are not ready to hear it, for to do so would be pronouncing false truths.*

What this means is that you, personally, have some knowledge of White Magick, and when will you have finished reading this book, you will have much more. But since every person is unique, you have to understand that not everyone shares your passion for Magick. Not all are open-minded in understanding and applying the Universal, Cosmic and Spiritual Laws.

It is more than certain that sooner or later you will want to get out of your loneliness and exchange your opinions about witchcraft with others. If only to seek answers to your questions or better yet, to find partners, witches with whom you could work together. Do not try to convince the weak-minded that you are right, you will needlessly waste your time and energy. If the occasion presents itself, do not say a word and know how to recognize in your heart that not all are at the same level of spiritual evolution. When these people finally decide to awaken and advance, like you, to a higher level of consciousness, they will come to you, but not before.

THE POWER OF THE VERB & INCANTATIONS

To successfully achieve a practice of sorcery, you will always need to fuse your entire witch powers into a single gleam, focused and trusted straight to the point. You must combine your will with your creative force of imagination and visualization, all strengthened by you are an unwavering faith that you will obtain what you desire. All you have to do is include the power of the verb and the incantation and your magick will be complete.

The verb used in witchcraft is called incantation. If a thought is capable of producing admirable effects and creating manifestations, so is the verb. It remains for you to understand how to use it for your own personal purposes. First, know that consciously verbalizing a specific sentence will have a significant impact in the invisible and subtle planes. That is why decent witches know that impurities should never be voiced wildly, because speech is indeed a form of energy and this energy can be creative as well as destructive.

In most cases, practitioners of White Magick will combine along their magickal powers, the force of the verb made of consecrated words that will constitute the incantation to be pronounced during rituals. By applying the 9th principle of witchcraft, the creative verb, you will possess all the necessary tools to accomplish all your occult experiments and magickal spells.

When a witch properly aligns herself with the appropriate frequency during a ritual, when she uses, in addition, the power of the verb and the incantation in order to build a vortex of energies that will be associated with the very nature of the ritual in question, it will trigger a delicate mechanism that will manifest the will into facts. An occult force will be launched into the Universe, and it will have no choice but to accomplish what it was intended for. However, beware of the Law of Triple Return because if this force does not hit its target, it will return to you immediately.

Incantations serve several purposes. First, as I have merely demonstrated to you, an incantation is a reflection of your will; it can produce a very powerful subtle force when pronounced appropriately and not lightly. You have to believe it! But even more, chanting a phrase specially conceived over and over again, like a mantra, will also allow you to intoxicate and alter your current consciousness to align with specific waves of a given energy. If, for example, you practice a ritual for love, repeating an incantation over and over will transport you to a completely different atmosphere; you will be able to connect to the energies conducive to love and, as a result, your ritual practices will simply increase tenfold. Here I give an example for love, but this principle is applicable to all actions of witchcraft, whatever they are.

The ideal incantation is one that holds a certain rhythm. The majority of witches find it is essential that it be rhymed and that is why they believe their incantations must be built by applying this necessity. Indeed, you will notice that by using rhythmic verses, these will have some impact on your psyche as they will be able to reach the depth of your mind. Here is an example:

Solar protection I hereby require,
From Knights of Light in armor,
Confusion I cast away and banish,
For I am protected by this wish,
Shadows are now a past fight,
For my will shines bright!

You see, in addition to being rhythmic and effective; the use of verses is also aesthetic. When you have to compose your own ritual incantations, you will certainly have to put a little effort into it, but these efforts will be rewarded, because any energy you deploy for a ritual can be used to make it manifest itself. Indeed, the energies that you will accumulate and launch into the Universe at the final moment of an action performed through practices of witchcraft will begin to be stored from your initial intentions as well as when you build your incantations.

SECOND PART

Preliminary Preparations

CHOOSING YOUR WITCH'S NAME

As you are now a witch in the making, the first step you need to take before going any further is to choose your magickal name. By carefully applying the six rules that constitute the pillars of witchcraft, that is, by developing the witches' six powers, all combined with respect for the 20 fundamental principles that we have seen together previously, something new has slowly sprouted in you. You began to develop your own magickal personality.

Some will say that adopting a witch's name is futile and unnecessary. I agree with that. It is not totally required to have one. However, know that choosing a witch name can be both as pleasant as it is important, from a psychological and occult point of view. Allow me to explain.

The magickal name is intended to define the occult personality of the practitioner of the Art. Adopting a witch name will represent you, as a unique individual practicing White Magick. Put differently, if you had to define yourself in one word, for all your witch qualities and powers, your *motto* or magickal name would be the right and perfect definition. The act of baptizing yourself with a name specially chosen to practice witchcraft will make it easier for you to detach yourself from your everyday personality. When you put on your ceremonial clothes and enter your magick circle, you are no longer he or she, son or daughter of him or her. No, you suddenly become Apollonius or Amaethon the sorcerer, Inanna or Melusine the witch!

In your day-to-day life, you may be a student, an office clerk or a programmer. It doesn't matter. For when the time comes to indulge in your Art, you will have to put all these considerations aside to detach yourself completely from the person you are and whom others know. You will immediately forget all your daily worries and obligations by putting on a completely different identity; the witch you truly are.

Your name should first and foremost express goals or qualities that you seek to acquire as a practitioner of White Magick. So which name to choose exactly? Your personality, your choice. I will not provide you examples of magickal names because I absolutely want your choice to remain personal and not to be influenced by anyone, nor even by me. You can be inspired by myths and legends, by antiquity, by your zodiac sign, your birth planet and the stories surrounding it.

To help you find your Magickal name more easily; I put here at your disposal this small process of numerology.

For example, you can add the numbers corresponding to the letters of your first and last name in order to obtain a numerical value, which can then be assigned to corresponding analogies. Use the following diagram to undergo your own tests.

1	2	3	4	5	6	7	8	9
A	B	C	D	E	F	G	H	I
J	K	L	M	N	O	P	Q	R
S	T	U	V	W	X	Y	Z	

Once you have obtained the total number, use what is called the *theosophical reduction*. This technique consists of reducing the number found in its simplest expression, and so on, until it is equal to or less than the number nine. Here is an example with my own name whose result will be the number four.

MARC   ANDRÉ   RICARD

4+1+9+3 + 1+5+4+9+5 + 9+9+3+1+9+4
(17)   (24)   (35)

17 + 24 + 35 = 76
7 + 6 = 13
1 + 3 = 4

Number obtained after theosophical reduction : **4**

If we look at some astrological and kabbalistic matches, we discover that the number four corresponds to the planet Jupiter and the Sephira Chesed.

1. Akâsha   —   Kether
2. Zodiac   —   Hochmah
3. Saturn   —   Binah
4. Jupiter   —   Chesed
5. Mars   —   Geburah
6. Sun   —   Tipheret
7. Venus   —   Netzah
8. Mercury   —   Hod
9. Moon   —   Yesod

All that remains is to consult books dealing with kabbalah or astrology and mythology in order to find names corresponding to the associations related to this Sephira or even, linked to the planet as well as all the legendary names attributed to it. If this method still does not satisfy you, then invent one for yourself! Yes, indeed, your magickal name can just as easily be the fruit of your imagination alone. But in any case, remember that it will always have to evoke in your mind this feeling of the unknown, this sense of magickal power and wisdom. For in fact, the magickal name can in addition, be used as a word of power; your personal strength as a practitioner of the White Art. It will soon become one of the keys to your deep psyche when you use it for this purpose. By pronouncing it aloud or silently, it will be of appreciable help to set in motion your magickal power and to align yourself with the waves conducive to a ritual. Thus, you can adjust certain rites as you wish by including a special part accordingly to your word of power to evoke and stimulate your own personal strength.

I have been asked, if not often, whether it is possible to alter the magickal name over the years, when it seems obsolete to us. Know that a magickal name symbolizes your personality as a practitioner and that it can indeed change. Some stipulate that a magickal name should get replaced as often as a new magickal goal is reached. However, I do not recommend modifying the name because it took time and effort to determine and decide on the latter, in addition to all the meaning and strength that this one will have stored as a name of power. If, on the other hand, you are truly determined to change your name, do so, but remember it will take time for it to become as powerful as your previous one.

Before closing this chapter about magickal names, I must advise to you that it will be an integral part of your witch personality, and as a result, that you should not choose it hastily. From now on, take all the time you need to think about your future name. The effort is well worth the result.

THE WITCHES' ALPHABET

THERE is in Magick a multitude of special characters and alphabets used by many practitioners in the implementation of their Art. Among these, we have the runes of Honorius, more commonly known as the Theban alphabet. These are the magickal characters that you will use throughout your White Magick practices.

A majority of witches estimate that this type of writing dates back thousands of years. Others agree that it would be a form of symbols related to the Enochian writing. For my part, I do not share this last opinion, but in any case, this ancient alphabet goes back a long way in a forgotten past. It is more than likely that it is a vestige of a very remote era.

You will therefore use these runes for all your writing needs, whether it is to transcribe incantations or when making charms and talismans, as well as to write your magickal name on your tools when you get to the stage of making them for frequent use during your witchcraft workings.

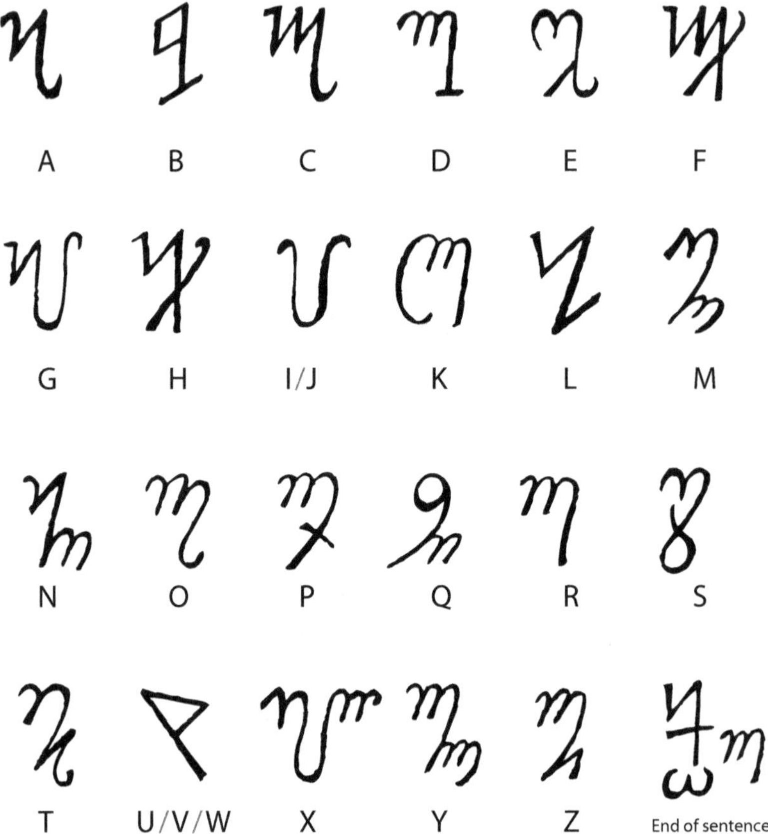

The Witches' Alphabet

In addition, I would like to point out that it is not necessary to learn this magickal alphabet by heart. However, if you take the trouble to study and assimilate it, you will be much more inclined to transcribe long incantations with this type of writing. Now, if you have a friend who practices magick with whom you can train, you can both exercise writing each other short sentences to try to read them correctly afterwards, without resorting to the following table. In this way, you will make giant strides while making it just more pleasant.

Finally, among other utilities, as these runes are reserved specifically for witches if ever, for any reason, someone was to discover your magickal material, you would at least have the assurance that your writings would not be compromised nor exposed. In this regard, your secrets will be protected and safeguarded. Indeed, you will see how easy it is to hide and conceal information through this alphabet.

CEREMONIAL CLOTHES

WE have now arrived at one of the most controversial subjects in the field of witchcraft. Many witches claim that it is essential to follow tradition by the book and to perform Magick completely naked. The reason for this resides in the thought that a garment could constrain or even stop the emergence of the practitioner's magickal powers. Of course, you will understand that this kind of thinking makes no sense. The power of witches is not tangible, it is invisible and timeless; it is an inner force. How then could a garment stop a magickal action? It simply cannot. Yes, clearly, uncomfortable clothing could however, eventually annoy and distract you.

Aside from a certain passage in the *Charge of the Goddess* associating nudity with freedom, there will always be a handful of purists to assert that since witchcraft is a return to the sources of nature and Universal energies, the fact of operating completely skyclad simply symbolizes the human being in its humble, most simple and purest original aspect, as nature conceived it. These are the only reasons that I think would suggest practicing Magick stark naked.

In any case, in a modern context, most witches tend to lean towards wearing the robe or the tabard. Simple and ample, so as not to obstruct movements, they seem much more appropriate. In addition, just putting on your robe every time you are about to perform an act of witchcraft, will serve as a psychological stimulus aimed at immersing you in the state of mind required for your magickal operations. This is the real purpose of the ceremonial robe.

As I mentioned, some people will want to follow the tradition and undress at all costs. Others will decide for the ceremonial robe. Finally, those who remain will choose neither of these options and will keep their everyday clothes. Please, do not prevent yourself from practicing White Magick because you do not yet possess your ceremonial robe. I have often been questioned about whether it is mandatory to make this type of magickal garment. No, the robe or the tabard is superfluous. Know that nothing is, so to speak, obligatory in Magick. As a result, always practice White Magick with this deep sense of freedom. I am only a guide for you, and I reveal to you the true processes. It is up to you to follow my advice or do what you like. What remains important is that you are comfortable with your own personal choices. Remember the witch's word; if it feels good to you, then it must be good.

It would be a good idea to always be clean before you put on your magick robe and stand in front of your sacred altar. By cleanliness, we obviously understand that it is a question of having purified your physical and psychic body beforehand so as not to taint your ritual garment with bad vibrations. In this regard, there are in some books of Ceremonial Magick, such as *The Key of Solomon the King*, very precise and ritual ways to prepare body and mind before wearing the magickal robes. As far as we are concerned, a magickal bath or, at least, a quick but conscious shower will do the trick. Refer to the chapter of magickal baths for all the details about these techniques.

Having now clarified the subject, all you need to know is how to make your ritual robe. I do not advise you to buy it, but rather to make it yourself. You will see, if you have any facility to use a sewing machine, you will find it very pleasant as a future project to realize.

Tau Robe   Simple Tabard

For those who want to go with simplicity, then opt for a simple tabard. In its most rudimentary form, this robe is simply a long piece of fabric folded in half with an opening for the head and arms, like a poncho whose sides would have been sewn to the bottom. If on the contrary, you feel up to it, then go for the Tau robe. As the name suggests, it has the shape of an elongated 'T'. The latter is most commonly worn by practitioners of the Art; both for witches and ceremonial magicians.

The more you put into it, the more satisfied you will be with the result obtained. If desired, you can also add a hood to get more impersonality during rituals. This is again at your sole discretion.

Finally, as to what material your future magick robe will be made of or what color should it be, it is up to you. Of course, traditional clothes will be made of universal white or black; everyone's favorite choice. If on the other hand, you want to put a little more color, then do so! There are no rules to follow in this area.

When you have finished your robe, you can then embroider on the hem or at the chest level your witch's name, using the Theban alphabet. You can even add other magickal symbols of your choice. As this garment is most personal to you, it is appropriate to decorate it at your image according to your intuition and personal tastes. When you wear your robe, you will use the rope called *cingulum* to bend your waist. We will come back to this soon in the chapter dealing with magickal tools.

Always store your robe or tabard in a place away from the profane and avoid, as much as possible, that it comes into contact with foreign hands. This garment is for you and you only. Finally, one last remark is necessary. Never wear this garment during social activities. Only endorse it when performing a magickal action and never under any other circumstances.

WITCHES' PERSONAL JEWELS

BEFORE going any further, I would like to mention at the outset that this chapter is completely optional. You are under no obligation to pursue, nor apply the subsequent explanations. On the other hand, if you want to observe somewhat the tradition, then the following may prove interesting and suit you in some way.

Many witches believe there are practical reasons to wear jewelry when someone is engaged in witchcraft. Some will, among other things, grant a power of fascination to their jewels, therefore allowing them to obtain a certain unspeakable influence on the people they meet in their daily lives. By fascination, one must understand an effect of amazement and hypnotic charm; to fascinate in the sense of subjugating others by the complexity and oddity of this type of artifice.

Moreover, it is also believed that these jewels possess magickal powers as an accumulator of occult power when they are regularly worn as talismanic objects, amulets or good luck charms. Obviously, this can be most truthful if a piece of jewelry, such as a ring, a bracelet or a pendant, was consciously created and charged with a specific and appropriate technique.

Either way, you surely have personal ornaments that you cherish and wear regularly. Perhaps you have also given certain virtues to your jewelry, such as luck, good fortune or protection. In short, we will now see some articles together that the witches wear. Then, if you feel like it, you can always do the same.

The bracelet

The bracelet is considered by traditional witches as a symbol of recognition between followers of the White Art. By this simple means, they recognize who they are, and who shares this magickal and spiritual path. Imagine, if all witches wore one, it would be so easy for you to know who shares your ideology and your sacred principles of magickal life. It would be all the easier for you to get out of the anonymity and isolation of the solitary way of which the vast majority of practitioners belong.

Of simplistic manufacture, sometimes even coarse, the bracelet is usually made of metal, either copper or silver. Normally, the inscriptions engraved on them are the magickal name of the bearer, the symbol corresponding to the cell of which he is a member, namely his coven as well as his rank. Of course, since I know that most of you are solitary witches, your bracelet could merely include the runes that constitute your magickal name, as well as personal symbols like your astrological sign, a Latin motto or from a magickal language such as Enochian, for example: *Oma Iadnah*, meaning 'to understand knowledge', etc.

If one day you decide to form your own witch coven, remember that a certain uniformity will be desirable, both for ceremonial clothes as for bracelets.

Rings

Rings are very common among witches. Some will appreciate these being the most bizarre or complex and decorated with precious or semi-precious stones in order to bring on an aura of mystery and unknown to their person. As with the bracelet, a majority will engrave their magickal name, while others will opt for runes or any other symbol of power. Practitioners of the Art also pay particular attention to the metal used because of its properties and the beneficial influences they bring. If necessary, consult the chapter on correspondences to find out more about them.

It is said that metallic jewelry inhibits the conductivity of occult forces deployed during rituals. In this regard, many will strictly observe this rule and remove any metal object from their person before entering the magick circle. If you think it makes sense, then do it. However, it is my opinion that this is untrue and personally, my ritual practices have never been diminished in any way because I was wearing rings or any other ornamentation.

The pendant

The pendant is probably the most appreciated among all practitioners of the Art. Usually, it will be a pentagram, the five-pointed star — the magickal symbol *par excellence*. However, it can also be made of a precious or semi-precious stone embedded in a small metal frame. Do not hesitate to consult a book dealing with the properties of stones to determine the influences you would like to benefit from if you choose to wear a stone as a pendant or amulet.

All these jewels should ideally be exorcised and then specially consecrated your own way during a waxing moon before you can wear them and benefit from their influences. You can proceed to this dedication act for all your ornamentations, one after the other.

MAGICKAL TOOLS OF THE TRADE

H ERE comes the most interesting part of all the preliminary preparations. In order to be able to carry out all your magickal operations and practices of witchcraft, you will sooner or later need to possess a complete set of tools specifically prepared for your ritual workings. We will see which are the main magickal instruments of the Wicca tradition that you will first have to familiarize yourself with, and, eventually acquire and consecrate in the near future.

Having that said, if you do some research on Magick, you will find that just about every esoteric discipline has an arsenal of instruments. The purpose of these magickal tools is easily explained; they are in fact the true auxiliaries of witches. They serve to store, manipulate and direct more adequately the elemental and subtle energies manifested during rituals and ceremonies.

There are, among other utilities, instruments dedicated to represent and invoke the forces of the four Elements, namely: Earth, Water, Air and Fire. To the latter, a fifth could be named, the Element of Spirit or Akâsha. These Elements have a highly prized place in Magick because they constitute the primordial forces of all life forms in the Universe and, above all, of Mother Earth. Without the contribution of these elemental forces, nothing could exist. That is why practitioners of White Magick honor and give thanks to them on a daily basis; they recognize the function and importance of these Cosmic energies.

On the other hand, the same is true of those, like me, who believe that magickal tools are, strictly speaking, optional, in the sense that true magick power comes from nowhere else but yourself! An experienced wizard would therefore be able to do without it if he wished. In this regard, I must make the following remark to you in order to ensure it permeates your conscience, today and forever:

Magickal tools are there to help and assist you in your tasks to manipulate the invisible forces of nature. Although these instruments have their own qualities and properties, never forget that it is not the tools that produce the results, it is you and none other than yourself by applying the six magickal powers of white practitioners:

THE TRUE MAGICKAL POWER IS IN YOU!

I had to share that with you, because my personal experience tells me that a large majority of uninformed people mistakenly believe that possessing all the magickal tools will make them powerful witches, even if they do not apply the six fundamental powers of White Magick. You will understand, of course, that such a reasoning can only be false.

Surely your magickal tools will inevitably be powerful allies only, and on the condition *sine qua non*, that they are used in concert with your own personal strength; this formidable magickal power, that has been conscientiously developed by rigorously applying the powers of witches who constitute the six pillars of witchcraft. If you manage to integrate this precept in your practices and throughout your coming magnificent magickal career, then your tools of the Art will be able to render you a valuable service, rest assured.

On the other hand, it is also possible that what you will learn in this book about magickal tools may not coincide exactly with what you might have seen on the subject in the past. I have tried to provide you with the most accurate information possible according to the oldest and most distant Wicca traditions. In a modern context, if you believe that some indications may not be necessary, especially with regard to the runes to paint on the magickal tools, then do not do it. However, those who want to apply the tradition will find everything they need to act like their peers of the times of the past, the witches of time old.

One last thing before going any further, never forget that your magickal tools are only used to practice White Magick and they will be dedicated for this purpose only. You must never use them for mundane uses under any circumstances. When you don't need them, store them in an appropriate place until a new opportunity arises. Finally, know that you do not need all these tools at once! Go one at a time, corresponding to your budget, but more importantly, according to your needs of the moment. The others will be added as your magickal practices become more demanding.

Here now are the traditional tools. As you will soon see, all of them have their usefulness.

☆ The Altar

Granted, the altar is not a tool strictly speaking. It is, however, the centerpiece, the epicenter of all the occult works you will undertake. The altar represents the foundation, the ultimate sacred base of your magick where all elemental and Universal energies awakened and invoked during magickal rituals and ceremonies come together. It is a place of transformations in front of which you will honor the God and the Goddess. We could even, knowingly, add that it symbolizes the nerve center of every act of witchcraft.

It is customary for the altar to be placed in the center of the magick circle, facing the rising sun, in the East. This is the location that most witches choose today. However, others will choose instead to place it in a northerly direction because of the analogy with the Earth Element. Wicca being considered by all practitioners to be the religion of the Earth; this also makes a lot of sense. Whether you place your altar facing East or North, it is still up to you. Remember

Magick can be flexible, and what you think feels right will be. The only thing I can recommend to you is to try both directions in turn to discover which one suits you best.

Once you are ready to use your altar concretely as a place of meditation and Magick, all you have to do is determine which item you would like to properly place on it. Never be limited by what you might have been told about it, for technically you can place all the magickal paraphernalia you want, including your tools, candles, God and Goddess effigies, flowers, stones and crystals, other sacred objects, etc.

Witche's Altar

Your altar is your sanctuary; it is therefore extremely personal to you. It is in this vein that you should ideally arrange it according to your tastes and the way that will seem most appropriate to you. In addition, as it also symbolizes the ultimate point where the elemental forces, the five Cosmic Elements (Spirit, Fire, Water, Air and Earth) come together, make sure you always have a physical representation for each of these Elements on your altar. All must be present or not at all, without exclusion. In the sense that to avoid imbalance, if some Elements were not represented, then none should be; they can never be separated from each other. With this in mind, you might also like placing the magickal tools as much as possible in front of their own Elemental Watchtowers; the cup of Water to the West, the incense for the Air to the East, etc. To offer you a starting point, I give you here an altar layout you can use or modify.

There is a last very important point that I absolutely need to mention. Remember, your altar symbolizes a sacred place dedicated to the God and the Goddess. It goes without saying that it must be approached and used with respect and diligence. Please, never use it for social activities, such as using it as a dining table, working or simply to lean back or rest your feet! I think I have been quite clear. A place where the Great Old Ones are worshipped should be treated the same as the gods themselves...

How to make this item:
The first consideration to take: the space needed to be at ease. A good altar must be large enough to receive all

your magickal tools, in addition to decorations and other objects you may eventually need to practice your charms, enchantments and spells.

There are no size rules to follow. This is up to your own tastes, your budget and the space you have in your workplace, because do not forget, you will need to move freely around it during rituals. The size of the altar does not matter. It can be high enough that you can stand in front of it, or even lower, as in the case of a bedside table. At that point, you will likely have to kneel to work properly.

As for the material your table will be made of; most witches opt for natural wood. Some believe an altar should not have any metallic parts such as screws or nails and the pieces should only be glued. Once again, if you think it is futile to dispose of your jewelry before proceeding with a ritual, as it was demonstrated in the previous chapter, there is no reason why your altar should not have pieces of metal, especially if it was purchased in a furniture store.

The next step is cleaning. Indeed, it is recommended to clean your altar-table physically and psychically before using it, as well as from time to time so that it remains always pure. While you are washing the altar, visualize at the same time that all the impure energies contained in your furniture are dissipating. There are not a hundred ways to do so. A little soap and water, your visualization and it is done.

Finally, if desired, cover your altar with a clean tablecloth. Many will prefer white fabric on which they will embroider a pentagram. If you prefer, go for a colored tablecloth according to your own personal criteria, blue, red, green or black, etc. Having followed these last instructions, you will possess a real and respectful magickal altar.

☆ The Athame

Athame, commonly referred to as a black-handled knife, is by far the most popular traditional magickal tool among all witches. It is the personal symbol of your Art and of the God, and therefore deserves to be carefully chosen and treated with the utmost care.

Used primarily to trace magick circles, to pierce and eliminate negative energies and to perform certain acts of consecration, the athame is a purely ritual tool, in that it will never be used as a knife to cut or engrave. For this purpose, there is another type of blade to perform these last functions: the bolline. This is why many believe the athame's blade does not need to be sharpened, but only pointy.

Traditionally, the athame has a double-edged blade and a black handle where the magickal symbols corresponding to this tool will be painted or engraved. Incidentally, some witches will prefer a natural alternative by opting for the magickal symbolism of a knife whose handle will consist of an animal material such as a deer's foot or a horn. I think both options are quite appropriate. However, you will understand that such a knife with an animal part can be very expensive. The choice of a simple athame will be more than suitable.

This ritual tool symbolizes male strength. It is also interchangeable with the sword because both possess the same occult qualities and functions as well as the same elemental attribution, namely the Air Element. It should be noted that some believe rather that the latter is associated with Fire and that the magick wand is of Air. Personally, I associate both Wicca and Ceremonial Magick with the Athame or the Sword to the Air and the wand to the Fire Element, and I have always obtained, by these attributions, excellent results. Do your own research, rely on your intuition and choose the symbolism that suits you.

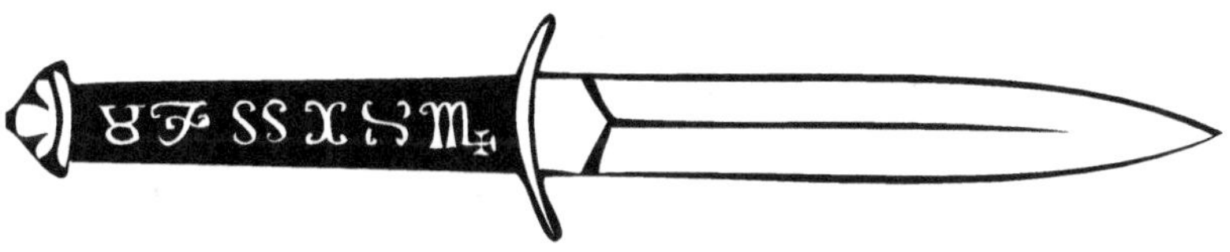

Characters on the first side of the athame

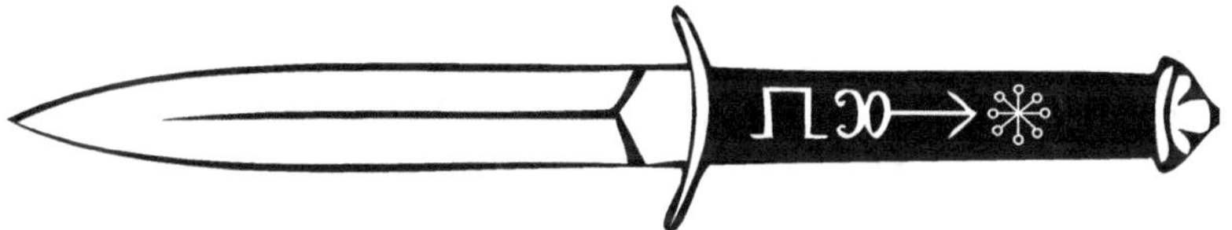

Characters on the second side of the athame

☆ *How to make this item:*

Start with a black-handled knife with a steel, double-edged blade. The latter must be new and have never been used before. The main idea is to find a knife that attracts you personally and that respects these indications. In case you fall in love with a knife whose handle is not black, you can always buy it. You will only have to gently sand the handle to soften it and then cover it with black paint.

The characters of the athame mean the following:

The Horned God; the power of fertility; the light half of the year.

The initial of the name of the God.

The Salute and the Scourge (with eight tails).

The Goddess as the waxing and waning Moon.

The initial of the multiple names of the Goddess in Hebrew character.

Sign of Scorpio; symbol of Death and of the Beyond, the counterpart of God as Lord of the Underworld; the dark half of the year.

The perfect couple.

The power always going forward from the Horned God or the conjunction of the Sun and the Moon.

The Eight Ritual Occasions; Eight Sabbaths, etc.

When you are in possession of your future athame, all that remains is for you to exorcise it in order to free it entirely from all psychic impurity by applying the *formula of exorcism* and consecrating it according to the *consecration formula of the athame or sword* that you will find in the next chapter. Finally, once this ritual is accomplished, paint with a new brush and white paint the specific runes of the athame on each side of the handle.

You can also provide a free space on the second side to enter your witch's name using the magick alphabet. Conclude your work by applying a thin layer of protective varnish would be advisable so that the characters cannot fade with the wear and tear of time, after many manipulations.

☆ **The Bolline**

Like the athame, the bolline is the witches' all-purpose white-handled knife. It is mainly used for engraving, carving, digging or cutting. In short, it is a utility knife used as any good knife should be. As the athame will only be used ritually, you will use your bolline for all your minor hands-on assignments, whether it is engraving symbols on candles, marking talismans on wood or metal, or, again, to cut while gathering your precious herbs, etc.

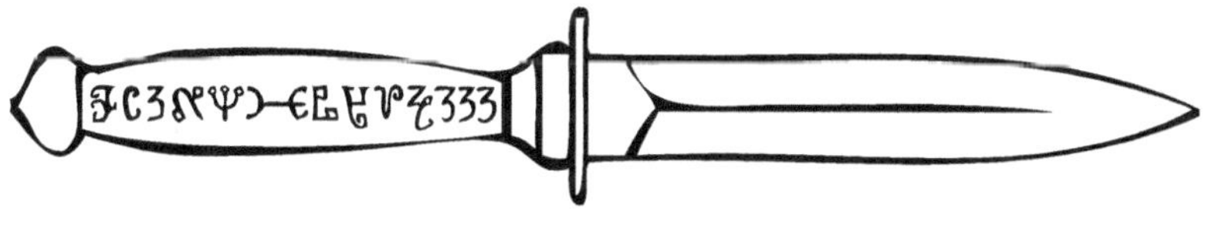

Characters on the bolline

Traditionally, the bolline looks in all respects like the athame with the only difference that the handle must be white. Obviously, as it is not always easy to find such an instrument, any knife, whether it has a single or double-edged blade will do. Some practitioners frequently use a knife whose blade has the shape of a crescent moon, like a sickle. The only thing that really matters and that you will have to comply with is the color of the handle and nothing else.

☆ *How to make this item:*

First, get a white-handled knife, regardless of its size and blade shape. It is very likely that you will have trouble finding one of the right color. If such is the case, choose any other knife that will appeal to you, knowing the handle can be easily modified at a later date and purchase it. You will only have to gently sand the handle to soften it and then cover it with white paint. As with the athame and with all your other tools, it must be new and never used before. Having accomplished this, you will have in your future bolline in your hands.

When you are ready to turn your new knife into a magickal tool, you will first exorcise it, then charge it properly according to the *consecration formula of the other tools.* Finally, once this ritual is complete, paint the special characters with black paint, as shown in the previous figure. You can also, if desired, write your witch's name on the other side using the magick alphabet.

✮ **The Cup or Chalice**

The magickal cup or chalice represents the Cosmic Element of Water. It is the symbol of feminine power *par excellence*; the great matrix of nature from which all things originated and to which all will one day return: the Goddess. The main function of the cup is to contain the consecrated wine of the libations which will be drunk at the end of the ceremonies. Some will also use it to contain the salt water from exorcisms at the expense of a bowl intended for the same use.

No matter how you use this tool, the cup is undoubtedly the counterpart of the athame, hence the union of these two magickal instruments beautifully compose the complementarity of the masculine and feminine principle, of the active and passive force, the God and the Goddess.

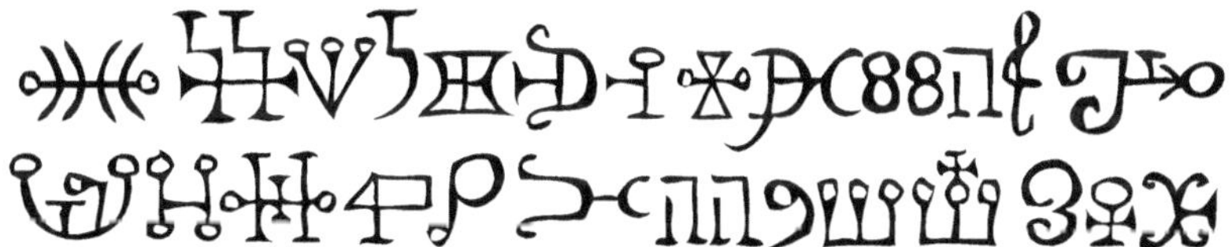

Characters of the cup

✮ *How to make this item:*

Purchase a new cup that has never been used. The material of which it is made does not matter, nor does its size. Only the appeal you feel for your cup counts, so go according to your personal tastes. In this regard, you can choose from a multitude of metal chalices made of silver, copper, brass or even wood, glass, crystal or vermeil. Some practitioners will even use animal horns. The only precaution to take, and this one is extremely important, is to make sure that no matter what material your new cup is made of, it is not porous. But even more, that the interior is well enameled, as in the case of the metallic chalices so that they do not become poisonous by reacting to the contact of certain liquids that you will have to drink afterwards. So, take all the required time to find the cup that suits you and choose it wisely.

When you are ready to turn your vulgar cup into a powerful and mystical tool of witchcraft, you will begin by exorcising it as usual in order to free it entirely from its psychic impurities. Subsequently, it will be properly charged according to the *consecration formula of the other tools*. Once the ritual is complete, paint the special characters of the chalice, as shown in the previous image. You can also, if you feel like it, write your witch's name on it, always using the magick alphabet.

☆ The Pentacle

The pentacle is of the Earth Element. According to tradition, it is the central piece of the altar on which are placed the objects that must be duly charged, whether they are magickal tools, bowls containing water and salt or any other item that you will have to use during your ritual practices of White Magick. However, some will rather place it to the North of their altars, knowing this is the cardinal point associated with the Element of the Earth.

One of its main functions, apart from consecrations, is to store and redirect the elemental energies of the Earth, while remaining a balancing agent of the other Elements. The use of the pentacle alone can serve, among other things, to center yourself when you feel unbalanced, as well as to reflect the bad energetic vibrations to expel them out of from your immediate surroundings.

Simple Pentacle   **Golden Dawn Pentacle**

☆ *How to make this item:*

This magickal tool is usually made of copper, ceramic or wood, but any natural material coming from Mother Earth will be excellent and perfectly suitable. Some practitioners will make use of a flat disc, while others will use one that will be slightly concave. You can follow the Order of Golden Dawn manufacturing method, which consists in dividing the disc into four equal parts and paint them respectively black, olive, rust and citrine.

Next, draw a white hexagram in the center of a circle and inscribe the symbols in black. Otherwise, to make a pentacle in its simplest expression, you can take a wooden disc and paint it with black, olive, rust or citrine paint or, again, by arranging the four colors at once as explained above. Thereafter gently draw a pentagram inside a circle with white or earth-toned paint.

Elaborate Pentacle

I offer here, as a complement, three different versions of pentacles. Study them carefully and select the one you like most. They are as good as each other and will have exactly the same effects.

The characters of the third pentacle mean the following: in the center, the pentagram, perfect magickal symbol and symbol of your Art. On the left, the symbol of the Horned God, on the opposite right, the crescent moons (waxing and waning) symbol of the Goddess. At the bottom, the Salute and the Scourge (S with an oblique bar) representing the complementary polarities of Severity and Mercy. At the top left, the downward triangle of the first initiatory grade, on the other side, the inverted pentagram of the second degree. Finally, the triangle pointing upwards, above the pentagram symbolizing the third Wiccan initiatory degree.

☆ The Censer or Incense Burner

The censer is used for fumigations, when you have to burn incense during magickal practices or periods of reflection and meditation. This tool is associated with the Cosmic Element of Air and should therefore, ideally, be placed to the East of your altar. The censer can be made of virtually anything, from a simple dish or metal plate to a raised tray resting on a tripod, to ecclesiastical incense burners mounted on chains.

Although some practitioners will go for simplicity, that is to say, a simple holder to burn incense sticks, it is, however, in my humble opinion that the best incense burner is the one used to burn charcoal pellets. The latter will be filled with about two centimeters of sand, as an insulating material (so as not to burn the surface of the altar) and the burning pellets will be placed on it. By using this type of incense burner, you will have much more choice when time comes to make your selection of incense. Indeed, knowing the vast majority of magickal incenses are composed of resins, herbs and essential oils, it will inevitably have to be deposited on embers.

No matter which model incense burner you choose, be careful using it and especially, when you manipulate it around your magick circle. Incense burners tend to get extremely hot!

Characters on the incense burner

☆ *How to make this item:*

Acquire a new incense burner. Exorcise it as usual in order to free it entirely from all psychic impurities. Then charge it according to the *consecration formula of the other tools*. Finally, once the ritual is complete, paint the special characters, as shown in the figure above. Your incense burner is now operational and ready to be used for all your magickal practices.

☆ The Cauldron

As such, the cauldron is a wider version of the cup. It thus symbolizes the feminine principle. This magickal tool is frequently associated with the cauldron of Cerridwen — the Grail of immortality. It is a symbol of renewal, rebirth and, of course, abundance as a feminine matrix. Due to its practicality, the cauldron will be used for multiple purposes. Whether it is a question of containing water, flowers, to burn incense or certain items during rituals, to prepare mixtures and philters, to practice divination as a magick mirror, in short, you will undoubtedly appreciate this highly functional tool because its use will be repeatedly solicited.

Your cauldron can be a simple bowl made of a resistant material like copper, brass or other, going as far as the very popular and ancient three-legged cast iron cauldron, which is by far the most satisfying of all. Be meticulous in the choice of your future cauldron, because having to use it frequently, it must be both robust, resistant, able to contain a good amount of liquid, and obviously easy to clean.

☆ *How to make this item:*

The cauldron requires almost no specific preparation, except to exorcise it and charge it, always according to the *consecration formula of the other tools*. This being done, you can use it immediately.

☆ **The Candleholders**

Magick lamps or candleholders are eminently important because of their profound symbolism as worthy Light bearers. This evidence leads us to associate them directly with the Solar forces. Lamps are perhaps one of the magick tools to which we give the least attention because of their simplicity and discretion, yet they will accompany you throughout your witch's career because of their necessity and essential functions.

Indeed, you should always have at least two candles permanently lit on your altar when you indulge in your practices of White Magick, that is, candles representing the God and the Goddess. Then, apart from the latter, you will be able to benefit from as many magick lamps to meet all your needs and requirements. Whether it is simply a matter of taking advantage of additional and adequate lighting so as not to work in the dark or to be able to read your grimoire perfectly in case you have to recite long incantations, whether you have to place lamps around your magick circle in front of each of the Elemental Watchtowers; the lamps definitely have a significant practical side.

Magick lamps are simplistic in design. Get as many as you need to carry out your rituals and ceremonies. Their appearance does not matter as well as their material. You can opt for metal candleholders, such as brass found almost everywhere in stores. Otherwise, you can buy them made of wrought iron, ceramics, wood, as long as they please you and your budget allows it. My only recommendation on this subject would be to try, as much as possible, to have some consistency when you make your choice. What I mean is that, at the very least, try to have an identical pair of candleholders for those who will hold the candles of the God and the Goddess. The rest is up to you.

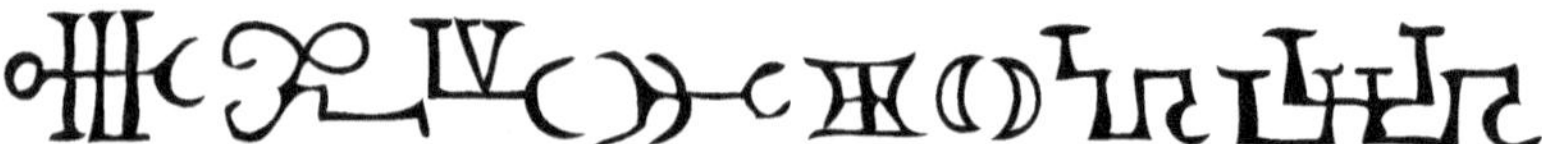

Characters appearing on the candleholders

☆ *How to make this item:*

Start by getting your candleholders. It is not necessary to buy them all at the same time. You can always add a few over the months and years, and then prepare them as prescribed when the need arises.

Then exorcise the lamps in your possession, one after the other, following the exorcism formula of the next chapter in order to free them from any psychic impurity. Following this, charge them in turn according to the *consecration formula of the other tools*. Finally, paint with your new brush the runes specific to candleholders. Your magick lamps are now ready to serve.

☆ The Book of Shadows and the Quill Pen

The grimoire is a real work manual commonly known as the *Book of Shadows*. Consider it a living thing, for like you, it will grow as you walk the path of White Magick. This is where you will record all your rituals, ceremonies, Sabbaths, incantations and magickal recipes of the most diverse before undertaking them.

This logbook is your personal book to transcribe everything related to your magickal practices. *It is intended exclusively for your eyes only*. Write it in the way you think is most appropriate. There are no rules to follow in this area. You will be able to deposit all the results of your magickal development exercises, when you train your six witch's powers. In this way, it will be easy for you, over time, to see how fast you are progressing and under what circumstances you have achieved results.

You can also create fact sheets on the rituals you will practice. For example, write down when the rite took place, such as the day and time, the duration of the latter, the lunar phase under which you worked, your physical condition, temperature, etc. Enter as many details you feel relevant and significant. Thus, when you find that your rituals have brought results or have failed, it will be easy for you to quickly go back and check under what circumstances the ritual was conducted. You will learn a lot from your experiences, and that is why you should always note them down carefully.

Characters of the Book of Shadows

This magickal journal is your companion along the way as well as a precious memory aid. Because from time to time, you may be unable to remember your recipes and the composition of your mixtures, as well as some important parts of the rituals you will practice or long incantations to verbalize. The more you magickally progress and the more experience you acquire, the more your grimoire will be filled with rituals, spells, recipes, notes, experiments and personal remarks. Always have your Book of Shadows handy on your altar or, if desired, use an easel that you will place near you.

As for the quill pen, with the grimoire, they are obviously indissociable; they form a pair. Get yourself a new quill pen and always use it only to write in your magick book or for your ritual writing needs. Some modern practitioners will use a pen with an integrated ink cartridge while those who wish to follow the tradition, just like witches of old times, will use a simple quill that must be dipped manually in an inkwell. This last alternative seems to me the most appropriate, despite the fact that it is a little more tedious to employ. However, you will have the option to use your own magickal inks that you have made yourself.

☆ *How to make this item:*
Buy a thick blank book like the sketchbooks we find in most art supply stores. Your future grimoire can be small and portable as well as voluminous. The important thing is that it contains enough pages to be of use for a long time. But do not worry if it gets filled quickly. Indeed, it is not rocket science, when the time comes, buy yourself a second grimoire and so on. In this regard, you may possess several grimoires, as much as you wish and as much as your needs require.

In due time, exorcise your notebook by following the exorcism formula prescribed in this book immediately after the *consecration formula of the other tools*. Finally, draw with your new quill pen (exorcised and consecrated) the pentacle and the runes of the grimoire on the front of the first page as well as on the back of the last. There will therefore be two pentacles in all, at the beginning and at the end of the magick book. Lastly, enter your witch's name in the center. Your Book of Shadows is now ready to be used to transcribe everything you desire.

☆ The Magick Wand

The magick wand is one of the most important instruments in Magick. Since time immemorial, it has been representative of all witches and wizards. There seems, however, to be some controversy over the Element associated with this instrument of the Art. I mentioned earlier that athame and the sword were associated with the Element of Air. On the other hand, some will say that the Wiccan tradition gives the same Element to the wand. We must pay attention to the deep symbolism of the magick wand to discover what is its true association so we may clarify this point with accuracy.

The wand essentially symbolizes will, strength and power. Now, by referring to the analogy of the Cosmic Elements, you will find that these three qualities are all governed by the fiery Element. There is consequently, no doubt that the ceremonial wand is indeed associated with the Fire.

Knowing this tool will allow the practitioner to keep under his influence the energetic Sphere for which it was designed and charged, you can easily understand that you will probably not have only one, but several wands, at the rate of one wand per goal pursued. Thus, you will be able to make wands for different occult actions. For example, curing diseases and banishing discordant or negative energies, evoking subtle Beings, Intelligences or demons so that they manifest, subduing the living or the deceased under your will whether they are human beings, animals, etc.

That said, although you can use an ever-increasing number of magick wands, you will be capable to produce a one-wand-fits-all, strictly speaking. It is this wand that I recommend you build in the first place, before all the others. The latter should therefore be conceived and charged in order to *manifest your will at all levels and towards all things.* In this way, it can serve you on various occasions, as we all know, the will is the driving force behind every action that takes place.

The magick wand is a real receptacle and power condenser. What you need to understand is that although the Wiccan tradition states that the branch that will make up your wand should have been cut off on a Wednesday at the hour of Mercury, it does not matter. What is essential, however, is that it is charged with and by your powerful will towards a specific goal. As a condenser, the wand will absorb and store the power conferred upon it. It is extremely important you remember that it is the repeated charging process that will give all the strength to your new wand and not the way it was built. It is hence, on that perspective that I will now continue my explanations.

Your wand can be made simple or very elaborate, including stones and crystals, wires, etc. Though, remember that only a specific wood whose nature is in accordance with the purpose of the wand must be chosen. That is, choose a wood that corresponds to the magickal work you want to accomplish with this instrument of the Art. In this regard, there are several properties of trees in the making of magick wands.

Traditional characters on the wand

Here are the main woods that will serve you throughout your occult practices:

Willow: The willow will probably be everyone's favorite, as it is an excellent accumulator agent and, as a result, it is an outstanding fluid condenser. Wands made from this wood can be used for multiple purposes. Select the willow tree to make your *all-purpose* instrument; thus, it will serve you on many occasions.

Hazel: The hazel is given the function of fulfilling wishes, whatever they may be. This type of wand is therefore suitable when you want to manifest your desires and cause changes in accordance with your will. Hazel is additionally a traditional wood used in witchcraft.

Elderberry: Wands produced from this wood will be excellent, even extremely effective to control elementary Spirits and demons because this tree vibrationally corresponds to the Saturnian Sphere.

Ash: Wands made from ash will be very good for accomplishing various purposes. However, the recommended use is to treat and cure diseases.

Beech or *acacia*: Beech and acacia are excellent trees for crafting magick wands for various purposes. You can use these trees if you are unable to procure yourself the other woods.

☆ *How to make this item:*

Crafting a magick wand can be extremely simple and easy and anyone can do it if they know how to apply some essential rules. Start by identifying the tree that best relates to the aims and functions your magick wand will need to fulfill. Then, when you have found the tree while walking in nature, cut a branch of about 1 to 2 centimeters in diameter and with a length of 30 to 50 centimeters, naturally as straight as possible and in the best conditions due to the growth of a single year. Tradition believes the ideal size would be the length between the middle finger and the elbow. This measure is equally acceptable.

Traditionally, cutting the wand should be done in accordance with precise astrological periods. It is not entirely necessary to respect this, but whoever has astrological knowledge about the periods ruled by planets (as explained in the chapter dealing with the calculation of planetary hours) should apply their knowledge to this end.

It is important to cut your branch with a new knife that will only be dedicated for magickal use. You will understand, of course, that we are talking about the bolline. If you do not have it yet in possession, you can always buy a new knife to cut your wand. Although the latter cannot be employed for profane use. It will have to be therefore buried if you wish to dispose of it, so that it does not fall into other hands.

Still with your magick knife, now strip off the branch of its bark and smooth it properly so that it becomes soft to the touch. The preliminary step is now complete. You currently hold a raw wand, capable of being charged by your power of visualization and will. To complete your work, exorcise your wand by applying the *exorcism formula*, followed by the *consecration and charge formula of the wand*. Finally, engrave or paint the traditional characters or any other symbol that will be in analogy with the powers of your magickal tool.

☆ The Sword

The sword is a masculine symbol associated with the Air Element. It is similar to the athame, because both are interchangeable and have identical functions and affinities. In this regard, we could conclude that the sword is a prolonged form of the athame. This ceremonial magickal tool, however, has a much more authoritarian character than the black-handled knife. It symbolizes, among other, things the righteousness of the practitioner who uses it as the absolute master of the magick circle and the Elements. The magick sword will be used in the same way as the athame.

☆ The Bell

The bell is used during ceremonies and rituals to mark time, as an opening and ritual closing; it announces the beginning or the end of a given cycle. It is stated, traditionally, that the bell also purifies the places where ceremonies are held and also helps to banish negative influences.

☆ Bowls of Water and Salt

These bowls will permanently appear on your altar. They are especially used for exorcisms and to purify any object during practices of White Magick. Water and salt are also used to consecrate and purify the magick circle. They are very basic and simple; two bowls of any material will do.

☆ The Cingulum

The magick rope or belt is called a *cingulum*. It is tied around your waist when you wear your ceremonial robe. It will also be useful for measuring the circumference while tracing your magick circles. In addition, you will also be able to bind yourself with it! Indeed, some techniques of witchcraft are referred to as binding. It is a way to stimulate the deep psyche of the practitioner in order to deploy his inner strength. During marriage unions within covens, one of the couple's hands is also bound together.

☆ *How to make this item:*

Do as most modern witches and buy yourself a skein of ribbon, traditionally red. Measure three rather long identical lengths (at least 3 meters) and exorcise them. Then all you have to do is tie a solid knot at one end and firmly braid your three ribbons together to get your magick rope. Complete the braiding with a second knot.

EXORCISMS & CONSECRATIONS OF MAGICKAL TOOLS

THE power to exorcize or consecrate is inherent in each of us. You do not have to be a great witch to achieve this. Having faith and conviction that our actions are sacred is enough for them to become so. Everything resides in the state of mind at the time these ritual acts are conducted.

Exorcisms have one and sole purpose, pure and simple: to purify and banish completely all psychic impurities impregnated in the work material of the officiant. However, it is therefore necessary, before using a raw material, to exorcize it properly so that it is able to become a magickal tool, a ritual accessory or any other specific object that will be used during practices of witchcraft.

Consecrations, for their part, are the logical continuation of exorcisms. Generally, one does not go without the other. The witch always starts by purifying the material and then consecrating it to give it a sacred or special status, from a magickal point of view.

It should be noted that the act of consecration has two distinct functions. The first is psychological. By dedicating a tool or an object that will be used as part of a magickal action, special importance will be given so that this object will no longer be seen in the same way; the latter having just been raised to a higher level. The practitioner's attitude in this regard will be modified, which will strengthen his will, creativity and confidence in all the magickal experiments he will undertake.

The second function is to alter the energetic body of objects during consecration. Indeed, not only witches, but also the majority of practitioners, magicians and occultists recognize that everything that exists physically also has an invisible shell or an energetic body designated as the astral counterpart. Thus, by consecrating an object and giving it a very specific utility and function, it is possible to make a change in the energetic body of this object or magickal tool. From this moment on, the latter will become personalized and vibrate differently from before, but even more, it will vibrate on the same waves chosen by the one who has duly charged it. This is where lies the secret of consecrations.

Now, when you have in hand some of your magickal tools, it will be time to exorcize them and then charge them. The first tool you will have to consecrate will be, of course, the pentacle, followed by the incense burner and the athame. Evidently, by reading the following formulas, you will understand that you will need the pentacle and the athame to carry out these magickal operations. However, when it is stipulated to use your black-handle knife, do it anyway (even though it is not yet properly charged). In the same way, during the exorcism and consecration of the pentacle, when it will be said to deposit the tool or the object on the pentacle itself, do nothing about it and move on with the formula. Then you can use your exorcized and consecrated pentacle to continue with your other magickal tools.

☆ **Consecration Formula of Water and Salt**

Here is the very first formula that should appear in your Book of Shadows. Before you can use water and salt for all your exorcism needs, you must first prepare them properly by consecrating them according to the method prescribed here.

With the bowl of water and salt on your altar, place the bowl of water on the pentacle and, holding your athame with both hands, hold the tip of the blade in the water and recite:

'I exorcize thee, O Creature of Water, that thou cast out from thee all the impurities and uncleanness of the Spirits of the world of phantasm. Mertalia, Musalia, Dophalia, Onemalia, Zitanseia.'

Remove the bowl of water from the pentacle and place the bowl of salt. Always holding the athame with both hands, hold the tip of the blade into the salt and say:

'Blessings be upon this Creature of Salt; let all malignity and hindrance be cast forth thencefrom, and let all good enter therein. Wherefore I bless thee and invoke thee, that thou mayest aid me.'

Finally, replace the first bowl on the pentacle and pour the salt into the water. Visualize a bluish light emanating from the bowl when the salt comes in contact with the water. Then say by placing your hands above the bowl:

'Yamenton, Yaron, Tatonon, Zarmesiton, Tileion, Tixmion. The union of consecrated Water and Salt purifies all.'

☆ Exorcism Formula

Having completed the consecration of your primary substances, water and salt, you can subsequently use them it to exorcize your magickal tools or any other object of your choice by the following formula. Remember to always exorcize in this way any matter that you will use during your practices of White Magick.

Burn in your censer a quality incense such as frankincense or any other incense you deem suitable for this purpose. Then take the object or substance to exorcize and place it on your pentacle. Then say by sprinkling it a few times with the consecrated salt water:

'Hear my will impure matter, thou are purified on this hour.
Negative energy I cast away, exorcized and free I now say.'

Then say, passing the object through the incense smoke:

'I exorcize thee once more, all wrong is banished.
Matter purified, obey my will, thou art cleansed.'

Hold the object with both hands and raise it above your head. Pause briefly, then place it back on the pentacle for a few seconds. The exorcism formula is completed. Repeat the formula for any other tools or objects you have to exorcize.

✮ Athame Consecration Formula

Although the traditional consecration formula stipulates that it must be practiced by a man and a woman, it was slightly modified so that any witch working solitary could charge the athame or sword without resorting to an assistant. The formula must be executed inside a magick circle. After consecrating the water and salt and burning a quality incense in the censer, take your athame (or sword) and place it on the pentacle.

Sprinkle the tool a few times with the mixture of water and salt. Then, pass it a few times in the smoke of the incense. Finally, replace the tool back on the pentacle. Put your hands on the athame with a light pressure and say the first conjuration:

'I conjure thee, O Athame (Sword), by these Names, Abrahach, Abrach, Abrahadabra, that thou servest me for strength defense in all my magickal operations against all my enemies, visible and invisible. I conjure thee anew by the Holy Name Aradia and by the Holy Name Cernunnos; I conjure thee, O Athame (Sword), that thou servest me for protection in all adversities; so aid me now.'

Once again, sprinkle the tool and pass it through the incense fumigation as before. Place the tool on the pentacle, put your hands on it and pronounce the second conjuration:

'I conjure thee, O Athame (Sword) of Steel, by the Great Gods and the Gentle Goddesses, by the virtue of the heavens, the stars and the Spirits who preside over them, may thou mayest receive such virtue that I may obtain the end that I desire in all things wherein I shall use thee, by the power of Aradia and Cernunnos.'

Take the tool in your hands and press it against your chest, then kiss the blade. Next hold it above your head to present it to the God and the Goddess. Take a brief pause. The consecration is completed.

Note:

It is said, according to the traditional method of consecration, that the athame must be near the naked body of the operator for a period of at least one month so that the latter can become impregnated with the aura of the practitioner. For example, by placing the tool under the pillow during the night, etc. If you feel like following tradition, I strongly encourage you to do so, although it is not absolutely necessary, it is still desirable.

☆ **Wand Consecration and Charge Formula**

This formula must be executed inside a magick circle. After consecrating the water and salt and burning a quality incense in the censer, place your wand on the pentacle.

Sprinkle it a few times with the mixture of water and salt. Then, pass it through the smoke of the incense. Finally, replace the wand on the pentacle. Place your hands on the tool with gentle pressure and say the following conjuration:

'I conjure the, O Wand, to serve me in all my magickal and occult endeavors, by the virtues that I will inculcate in you. Be a tool of power that will act as an extension of my will. I conjure the again by my strength to be propitious and to serve only to express and manifest the same will of mine.'

Once again, sprinkle the tool and pass it through the incense smoke as before. Place the tool back on the pentacle for a few moments, then continue with the charge of the wand.

The Charge of the Wand:

Hold your wand in your hand and focus on your will. Project your consciousness into your tool; you are now becoming the wand itself. Concentrate in this way for a few minutes, visualizing firmly that every time you hold this wand, it will immediately express your will and perform the latter so that everything you want to undertake and see realized will thus be manifested right away. Project your will in the wand with the highest possible intensity that your visualization can reach.

In order for your wand to remain active at all times and even until after your death, you will need to specify during your visualization that as long as it exists, its power will continue to increase day by day, and will express and manifest your will and power at all times, with every use. Your wand can therefore truly remain active and functional as long as it is not destroyed, if that is your wish, provided that it is clearly specified from the outset, during the first charge.

At first your wand will be active on the mental plane, then on the astral plane, and finally on the physical plane. Of course, to succeed in making a wand operating straight on the material level, you will have to frequently repeat the charge procedure I have just explained, by accentuating the ardor of your concentration each and every time. It is obvious that in order to obtain such a powerful magickal tool, it will depend on your ability to project your will and the degree of your visualization, as well as the goal entrusted into this wand. In any case, this authentic technique can only bring you excellent results if you take the trouble to follow these instructions and apply them conscientiously and meticulousness.

By following this principle, you will be able to craft as many magick wands as you want, while never forgetting to grant the specification and the nature of the action to your wand from the start, during the first charge.

)O(

☆ Consecration Formula for Other Tools

This consecration formula is used for all magickal tools except the athame, the sword and the wand. It must be performed within a magick circle. After consecrating the water and salt, and burning a quality incense in the censer, take the tool in question and put it on the pentacle. Place your hands on the magickal tool and then say:

'Aradia and Cernunnos, deign to bless and consecrate this (name the tool) that it may obtain the necessary virtue through you for all magickal act, of love and beauty.'

Sprinkle the tool a few times with the mixture of water and salt. Afterwards, pass it through the smoke of the incense. Finally, place the tool back on the pentacle. Put your hands on it again and continue:

> *'Aradia and Cernunnos, bless this instrument prepared in your honor. May it serve in my magickal practices, for good uses and for your glory.'*

Sprinkle the tool once more and pass it through the fumigation. Take the tool in your hands and press it against your chest, then give it a kiss. Hold it above your head to present it to the God and Goddess. Take a brief pause. The consecration is completed.

Notes about consecrating Magickal Tools

Tradition states that when a tool has just been consecrated, it should be used immediately. For example, following the consecration of the athame or the sword, the magick circle will once again be traced with the now consecrated tool. One will engrave some object after the consecration of the bolline, one will make a fumigation after having consecrated the incense burner, one will exhibit the pentacle or the wand in front of the four Elements, the four Elemental Watchtowers and so on.

It is not mandatory to follow this tradition if you do not see the need for it. However, it would be advisable to do so, if only in a purely symbolic way. In addition, it is also indicated that the magickal tools should be stored close to the place where you sleep and to manipulate them a little before retiring for the night, so that they become impregnated with your energy for at least a month. Once again, purists will follow these rules, but it is really up to you whether or not they hold any significance. If you ask for my humble opinion, then I recommend you do so.

No matter what you do with these indications, one thing remains very important. Once your tools have been consecrated, wrap them in a clean and exorcized cloth, preferably in a piece of white silk, and store them in a discreet, if not secret, place.

MAGICK CIRCLES: POWER LENSES

A CONCEPT comes up very often about Magick, without however being a precept. I am very frequently asked questions about those famous magick circles; how should I trace it? Is it a circle of protection? Are magick circles important or mandatory, etc.?

All those questions, too often raised, shows to what extent the matter is still relevant and how no one seems to have a real answer. Without further ado, I will reveal you what the functions of magick circles are and how a practitioner of the Art can make use of them.

The circle is above all a magickal symbol of the utmost importance. It represents a whole, the beginning and the end in perpetual cycles, the One. When one stands in the center of the circle, it symbolizes a mastery over the microcosm and the macrocosm — master of one's own Universe and of the grand Universe in which he interacts. He represents himself as the Divine power. He thus becomes at that precise moment the Light on all things.

Now, the magick circle, physically and immaterially speaking, is also used as a space of confinement or a lens of power in order to concentrate with intensity in one place all the forces and energies evoked by the officiant.

The reason why many people consider it a 'protective circle', is that the circle, seen as an energetic space, I prefer to say power lens, prevents the awakened forces from dissipating outside this delimited space, as long as the circle is properly traced according to the rules of the Art. So, yes, it is true to say that the circle will *protect* against energy losses.

Obviously, the circle will also possess its protective sense as a psychic barrier, preventing Entities and Spirits from trespassing, always, and on the sole condition that the latter was traced adequately, that is, not only physically by the hand, but on the three planes of existence simultaneously; physical, psychic and mental. Indeed, erecting a physical barrier will never do more than prevent intruders from the physical plane. An Entity living on the astral plane not governed by the Laws of matter can without difficulty penetrate the magick circle as easily as it can enter any dwelling. Consequently, to protect himself from the astral Entities, the practitioner will have to build a defense on the same plane of existence of the latter.

So, as I just mentioned, the most important thing to remember is that the circle can be drawn physically, with your athame, but even more, mentally, without twitching a finger. In this regard, it is therefore possible to trace it only by thought, supporting your visualization with a gesture of the hand, imagining you erect a powerful psychic and energetic barrier. The circle must remain constantly visible and present in your mind. No matter what you choose to do, both methods are excellent.

To summarize, we could define and simplify as much as possible the functions of the magick circle in two very distinct aspects. In practical Magick, the circle will protect against hostile vibrations coming from the outside, while from the inside, the circle will concentrate the energies evoked in this delimited space, thus forming a strong lens of power and a sacred workspace for the officiant.

In conclusion, the witch will draw a magick circle in order to create a sacred and pure space, free from all contrary vibrations, then, she will evoke the energies of the Universe that she wishes to be present with her, asking, among other things, the Elements to join the ceremony.

☆ Three Types of Magick Circles

Know there are several types of magick circles. Even though similar, there are many ways to trace them, or rather I would say, to charge them. These ranges from the simplest to the most complex. In a former book, I wrote there were at least three different ways to develop such confinement circles. There are others, but the following will be sufficient to give you a good overview of the possibilities.

Here are three types of circles that can be constructed by analogies:

A) Divine analogies: The circle is based on the divine correspondences to be invoked.

B) Planetary analogies: The circle is based on the correspondences, colors and fumigations associated with the planets.

C) Elementary analogies: The circle is based on the correspondences, colors and elementary fumigations, i.e.: circle of Fire, Air, Water and Earth. This is the type of circle that you will commonly use in witchcraft.

These types of circles are characterized as follows:

A) This circle is based essentially on divine representations, dedicating it mainly to deities, gods and goddesses. This is notably the type of circle obtained by the practice of the Lesser Banishing Ritual of the Pentagram.

B) This circle is constructed according to planetary correspondences, in analogy with the dominant planet in a specific ritual.

C) This circle is constructed according to the elementary correspondence of a given Element, whether it is Fire, Water, etc.

This being demonstrated, be aware that magick circles are not always required, at least as far as Ceremonial Magick is concerned, for a mage recognizes that by practicing the Lesser Banishing Ritual of the Pentagram (LBRP), her basic magick circle is already and automatically traced. However, in witchcraft, the tradition indicates (not in the obligatory sense) to always draw one and that these are essential at all times for any magickal action, whatsoever, in order to dedicate an adequate working space (to the God, the Goddess and the Elements) and to focus in one place the energies set in motion by occult rituals and experiments.

Although there may be as many variations as there are witches on how to trace a magick circle, here I offer you a traditional and ritual method to create your sacred space. The general idea that we find expressed among a majority of witches is that witchcraft being the religion of the Earth. Thus, when drawing the circle, they will evoke the Earth Element and will officiate with their altar facing North. Certainly, that's one way of looking at things. For my part, and at the risk of being criticized for my too complex rituals, I will present to you the way to trace a circle according to *elementary analogies*, which will make use of four pairs of Invoking and Banishing Pentagrams. Thus, the altar will be oriented facing the East and the four cosmic Elements will be invoked, in turn, to obtain a perfect balance. The attentive practitioner will notice a very great similarity between this technique and the Invoking Ritual of the Pentagram practiced essentially in Ceremonial Magick. You are free to use this technique or modify it according to your needs, such as using only the pentagrams of the Earth Element.

Ultimately, remember that when you make use of a magick circle, the circle drawn physically on the ground will only act as a mental support. You must be able to represent it in your mind at all times. Indeed, everything happens at the level of the practitioner's consciousness.

☆ Casting the Magick Circles

Having taken care to place all your magickal tools on your altar as well as all your necessary equipment to practice your rituals without omitting anything, you can then cast your magick circle.

Start by lighting the candles representing the God and the Goddess as well as the candle representing the Fire Element and burn some incense. You can, if desired, also light a candle at each cardinal point in front of each of the Elemental Watchtowers.

Approach the altar and kneel with respect and diligence.

Then consecrate the water and salt according to the usual consecration formula: *'I exorcize thee, O you Creature of Water...'*, etc.

With the water and the salt duly consecrated, begin to trace your magick circle with your athame (or sword) from the East to return to the East (or from the North to the North for some other practitioners), always in the direction of the Sun, thus walking clockwise. As you draw the circle, visualize electric-blue flames crackling on the ground along the line of your blade while saying (or just after):

'I conjure thee, O Circle of Power, that thou may be a place of love, joy and truth; a shield against all wickedness and evil; a boundary between the world of men and the realms of the Great Old Ones; a rampart and protection that shall preserve and contain the power that I shall raise within thee. Wherefore, I bless thee and consecrate thee, in the names of Cernunnos and Aradia.'

Return to the altar and replace your athame. Then collect the bowl of salted water and starting from the East, circumambulate sprinkling the perimeter. When back to the East, return to your altar and take the incense burner. In the same way, walk around the circle, incensing your workspace. Finally, take the candle of Fire and make last turn around the circle. Back in front of the altar, replace the candle, pick up your athame once more, and head to the edge of the circle facing East.

Using your athame, trace in front of you, in the air, an Invoking Pentagram of Air. Start with the upper right tip, as shown on the next page.

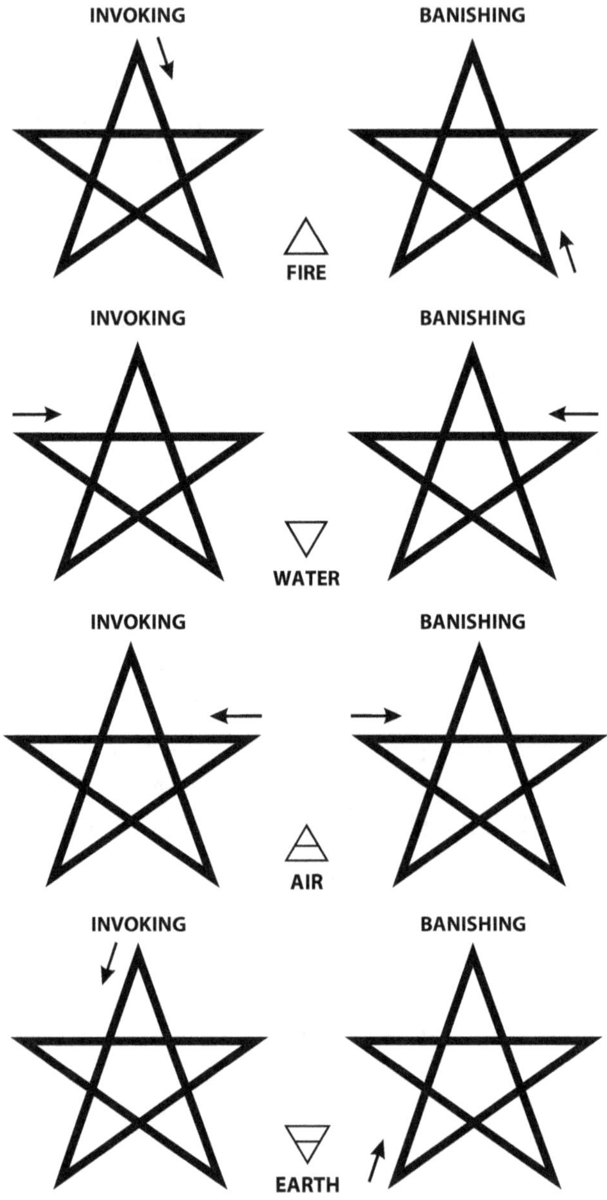

Invoking and Banishing Pentagrams

To help you trace the pentagram of the right dimension, use your body as a guide. Start at your right shoulder and trace the first side towards your left shoulder. Then go down to your right hip and then up to the level of your forehead. From there, descend to your left hip and complete the pentagram by returning to your starting point.

Visualize as you trace the pentagram, a flame gushing out of the tip of the blade, like the blazing fire of a soldering torch. This light must be visualized in an extremely bright electric yellow. While drawing the pentagram, say:

'Lords of the Watchtower of the East, Lords of Air; I do summon, stir and call thee, to attend my rites and guard this Circle.'

Head along the periphery of the circle to the South, trace and Invoking Pentagram of Fire and visualize it in a very bright red. Say:

'Lords of the Watchtower of the South, Lords of Fire; I do summon, stir and call thee, to attend my rites and guard this Circle.'

Head along the periphery of the circle to the West, trace and Invoking Pentagram of Water and say:

'Lords of the Watchtower of the West, Lords of Water; I do summon, stir and call thee, to attend my rites and guard this Circle.'

Head North and conclude with the Invoking Pentagram of Earth, in a very bright green, saying:

'Lords of the Watchtower of the North, Lords of Earth; I do summon, stir and call thee, to attend my rites and guard this Circle.'

Complete the circle and finally return behind your altar, always moving clockwise. Place your athame on the altar. Your magick circle is now drawn. You can then continue with your workings of White Magick or any occult experimentation you wish to undertake.

)O(

Note on circle exits:

If for any reason, you needed to exit your circle during a ritual or ceremony, take your athame and head North East. Starting from the ground, at the periphery of the circle, trace from left to right an entrance or a portal sufficiently wide and high enough so that you can pass through. As soon as you return, close the circle by drawing a line on the ground, from left to right, where the gate was, and seal once more the circle.

I do not recommend using this technique extensively, but if you cannot do otherwise, as in the case of an emergency, then the portal will allow you to do so without the risk of breaking the magick circle and dissipating energies.

)O(

✫ Closing and Sending the Circle back to the Universe

When all your magickal operations are completed and it is time to conclude them, the last step to be performed will be to properly close the circle and return (banish) all the energies from which they originate, that is, to send them to the Universe.

It is crucially important to never forget this final phase of a magickal action, otherwise the energies and vibrations invoked or evoked will dissipate in all directions and will remain in place even long after you have left your workspace.

Athame in hand, go to the edge of your circle to the East. Trace the Banishing Pentagram of Air. While tracing the pentagram, say :

'Lords of the Watchtower of the East, Lords of Air; I thank thee for attending my rites; time has come to return to your respective realms, I bid you hail and farewell.'

Head along the periphery of the circle to the South, trace a Banishing Pentagram of Fire, while saying :

'Lords of the Watchtower of the South, Lords of Fire; I thank thee for attending my rites; time has come to return to your respective realms, I bid you hail and farewell.'

Then head along the periphery of the circle to the West, trace a Banishing Pentagram of Water and say :

'Lords of the Watchtower of the West, Lords of Water; I thank thee for attending my rites; time has come to return to your respective realms, I bid you hail and farewell.'

Finally head North and trace a Banishing Pentagram of Earth, saying:

'Lords of the Watchtower of the North, Lords of Earth; I thank thee for attending my rites; time has come to return to your respective realms, I bid you hail and farewell.'

The elemental energies have been properly banished, and the circle is now closed. This puts an end the ritual practice. Extinguish all candles with your thumb and forefinger (without blowing them off), clean your altar properly and store your ritual robe and tools until the next occasion.

THIRD PART

Initiation to Witchcraft & Universal Vibrations

THE GREAT GOD CERNUNNOS INVOCATION

Great God Cernunnos, return to earth again!
Come at my call and show thyself to men.
Shepherd of Goats, upon the wild hill's way,
Lead thy lost flock from darkness into day.
Forgotten are the ways of sleep and night —
Men seek for them whose eyes have lost the light.
Open the door, the door which hath no key,
The door of dreams, whereby men come to thee.
O Mighty Stag, O answer to me!
Akhera goiti! Akhera beiti!

THE CHARGE OF THE GODDESS

Listen to the words of the Great Mother, who was of old also called Artemis; Astarte; Diana; Melusine; Aphrodite; Cerridwen; Dana; Arianrhod; Isis; Bride; and by many other names.

Whenever ye have need of anything, once in a month, and better it be when the Moon be full, then ye shall assemble in some secret place and adore the spirit of me, who am Queen of all Witches. There shall ye assemble, ye who are fain to learn all sorcery, yet have not yet won its deepest secrets: to these will I teach things that are yet unknown. And ye shall be free from slavery; and as a sign that ye are really free, ye shall be naked in your rites; and ye shall dance, sing, feast, make music and love, all in my praise. For mine is the ecstasy of the spirit and mine also is joy on earth; for my Law is Love unto all Beings. Keep pure your highest ideal; strive ever toward it; let naught stop you or turn you aside. For mine is the secret door which opens upon the Land of Youth; and mine is the Cup of the Wine of Life, and the Cauldron of Cerridwen, which is the Holy Grail of Immortality. I am the Gracious Goddess, who gives the gift of joy unto the heart. Upon earth, I give the knowledge of the spirit eternal; and beyond death, I give peace, and freedom, and reunion with those who have gone before. Nor do I demand sacrifice, for behold I am the Mother of All Living, and my love is poured out upon the earth.

Hear ye the words of the Star Goddess, she in the dust of whose feet are the hosts of heaven; whose body encircleth the Universe. I, who am the beauty of the green earth, and the white Moon among the stars, and the mystery of the waters, and the heart's desire, call unto thy soul. Arise and come unto me. For I am the Soul of Nature, who giveth life to the universe; from me all things proceed, and unto me must all things return; and before my face, beloved of gods and mortals, thine inmost divine self shall be unfolded in the rapture of infinite joy. Let my worship be within the heart that rejoiceth, for behold: all acts of love and pleasure are my rituals. And therefore let there be beauty and strength, power and compassion, honour and humility, mirth and reverence within you. And thou who thinkest to seek for me, know thy seeking and yearning shall avail thee not, unless thou know this mystery: that if that which thou seekest thou findest not within thee, thou wilt never find it without thee. For behold, I have been with thee from the beginning; and I am that which is attained at the end of desire.

SOLITARY INITIATION TO WITCHCRAFT

I MENTIONED to you at the beginning of this book that in a modern context, the initiation from witch to witch was no longer necessary. Incidentally, you should never stumble over this part of the tradition, as you will agree, you may have to wait a long time before you have the chance to meet a witch ready to make you a new initiate in the White Magickal Arts.

Traditions have existed since time immemorial and will continue to live from generation to generation. However, mentalities are also changing and evolving. What was once right and necessary may not be so today. What was once a well-kept secret has become a truth accepted by all. In any case, a fundamental rule has always been firmly rooted in witchcraft: respect for freedom. Having this choice and free will, you can therefore choose to wait to be initiated by a witch or do it by yourself, without further delay. The Old

Gods will not scorn at you if you make this big step alone, on the contrary, they will welcome you with opened arms.

There can be numerous reasons to initiate yourself on your own. It is quite possible, if not beyond all doubt, that you feel this attraction to the religion of the Earth and its noble principles of life; that you have this desire deep within you to unite with the forces of nature and the Universal energies or that you wish to join a circle of people who take precedence over respect for all creation by showing inner and spiritual growth. All these reasons are good, and I am sure that you also have yours, all of which are equally valid.

So your greatest desire at this moment is to become a witch? Do you want to practice the rituals and ceremonies of the past and honor the Great Ancients? Then practice the following ritual, it will be more than enough to properly initiate you to the White Art by yourself, without resorting to anyone.

My first recommendation is that you take the trouble to read the ritual a few times before practicing it. I ask you to do this so that you can fully understand what you are about to engage in. Take all the time necessary to grasp and assimilate the profound meaning of this initiation, for it is a very solemn act and of the utmost importance. If you do not feel ready, then wait for the suitable moment. For once you have been initiated and take the oath; it will be too late to go back. The Gods will never perceive you the same way again.

Dear practitioner to be, if you feel the time has come for you to bring out your true magickal personality, then go pure of heart and get prepared to experience one of the most important moments of your life.

☆ Preliminary preparations

Prepare your workplace properly and make sure it is clean. Unplug the ringtone from your phone and, if necessary, close the windows, to cut off outside noises. Now place all your magickal tools and candles on your altar and set the latter in the center of your sanctuary facing North. Indeed, for this ritual only, the altar will face North because of the association with the Earth Element.

You will also need for this ritual your cup filled with wine as well as an oil, any will do the trick, although an oil of consecration or blessing is even more appropriate.

Now, take a ritual bath or a conscious shower to purify yourself of body and mind (see the following chapter about magick baths for the complete procedure). Put on your ceremonial robe, if you have one, otherwise simply remain nude for the duration of the initiatory rite. Then approach the altar in silence and do a short meditation about the solemn act you are about to perform. When you are ready, begin the ritual.

The Initiation Ritual

Start by lighting the candles symbolizing the God and the Goddess as well as the one representing the Fire Element and burn some incense. You can, if desired, also light a candle at each cardinal point in front of each of the Elemental Watchtowers.

Now kneel before the altar with respect and diligence. Consecrate the water and salt according to the usual consecration formula. Afterwards trace your magick circle with your athame starting from North to North, always in the direction of the Sun. After having walked along the circle with the salted water (sprinkling it), the incense burner and the candle, and after having traced the Invoking Pentagrams and summoned the Watchtowers, that is, when the circle will be properly drawn, as prescribed in the second part, go back at the altar facing North.

Raise and spread your arms high in the air and say:

'I invoke and call upon thee, Great and Mighty Mother of us all, bringer of all fruitfulness; by seed to root, by stem to bud, by leaf to flower and fruit, do I invoke thee to bless this rite and to admit me into the company of thy hidden children.'

Take a brief pause and recite the *Charge of the Goddess.*

Then, still facing the altar, raise your arms once more and make the sign of the Horned God with both hands (index and little fingers extended, thumbs and middle fingers folded) and recite the *Great God Cernunnos Invocation.*

Briefly pause in silence and then continue:

'Gentle Goddess, mighty God; I am your child, now and always. Your breath is my life. Your voice, Great and Powerful Mother, and yours, Great and Powerful Father, speak within me, as they do in all your creatures, if only we could listen. Therefore, here in your Magick Circle, which stand between the world of men and the realm of the Great Old Ones, do I open my heart to your blessing.'

Meditate as long as desired on the presence of the God and the Goddess and on the profound meaning of your words. You can sit on the floor if desired. Open your heart to them and let yourself be bathed in their energies. After, head to the boundary of the circle to the East and say:

'Take heed, ye Lords of the East and of Air, for I (your magickal name) am properly prepared to become a priest (priestess) and a witch.'

Head South and say:

'Take heed, ye Lords of the South and of Fire, for I (your magickal name) am properly prepared to become a priest (priestess) and a witch.'

Head West and say:

'Take heed, ye Lords of the West and of Water, for I (your magickal name) am properly prepared to become a priest (priestess) and a witch.'

Head North and say:

'Take heed, ye Lords of the North and of Earth, for I (your magickal name) am properly prepared to become a priest (priestess) and a witch.'

Complete the circle and go back in front of your altar. Place your right hand on your heart and solemnly recite the witches' oath with sincerity:

'I, (your magickal name), in the presence of the Great Ones, do of my own free will and accord most solemnly swear that I ever keep secret and never reveal those secrets of the Craft which shall be entrusted to me, except it be to a proper person, properly prepared within a Circle such as I am now in; and that I will never deny these secrets to such a person if he or she be properly vouched for by a brother or sister of the Art. All this I swear by my hopes of a future life; and may my weapons turn against me if I break this my solemn oath.'

Bow before the altar, and then, taking the oil, anoint your fingertips and say:

*'I now sign myself with the Triple Sign.
I now consecrate myself with the oil.'*

Lightly anoint yourself with oil at the level of your lower abdomen, then on the right side of your chest, next on the left and finally on the lower abdomen one last time, thus completing the inverted triangle of the First Degree of initiation. Now moisten your fingertips with the wine and say:

'I now consecrate myself with wine.'

Touch yourself once again in the same places as before. Finally, give a kiss on your fingertips saying:

'I now consecrate myself with my lips.'

Trace the inverted triangle one more time and touch yourself again at your lower abdomen, then the right side, on the left of your chest, and ultimately at the level of the lower abdomen one last time. Next proceed to the final step.

Head to the boundary of the circle to the East, then South, West and North and say, while facing each Elemental Watchtower:

'Hear me, Great Ones of the East (South, West, North) and of Air (Fire, Water, Earth), I, (your magickal name), have been duly consecrated priest (priestess), witch and hidden child of the Goddess.'

Your initiation into the path of witchcraft is duly completed. Be proud of it because this is a great day! I therefore offer you all my congratulations, for you are now a true witch, son or daughter of the God and the Goddess!

THE SECRET OF MAGICKAL BATHS & OF THE PURIFICATION OF BODIES

To consciously practice Magick when one adheres to the Wicca tradition, is first and foremost to respect and direct the flows of energies or surrounding psychic currents. To be able to apply a voluntary pressure, therefore through our will, on the energies of nature that surround us, we must ideally be ourselves free of negative energies, which we also refer to in terms of vibrations, so as not to mishandle the energetic currents that are manipulated by means of rituals.

We are constantly surrounded by all kinds of vibrations and psychic emissions. They impregnate and permeate us without our knowledge and can even accentuate and influence our attitude and all our behaviors. To give you a clear and pictorial idea of this concept, imagine for a moment that all the air around you suddenly becomes scented.

Anywhere you set foot, you walk through these subtle and fragrant layers. In various places you will find different vibrations, positive and also negative or, as in this example, several perfumes. Some will be very pleasant and aromatic, while others will be heavy and dense, or even unbearable and nauseating.

What I want you to understand through this metaphor is that just like a perfume that adheres to your clothes, the subtle vibrations, on the other hand, infiltrate your psychic bodies. This phenomenon has always existed, but the majority people merely do not realize it.

Hence, to succeed in freeing yourself from negative psychic influences, a daily purification is necessary, but even more so, just before putting on your ceremonial robe in order to perform a magickal act. Indeed, you definitely do not want to carry with you in your magick circle, in the middle of your sacred sanctuary, contrary and unhealthy vibrations!

Although there are many methods to purify oneself, one of the most popular and effective is undoubtedly the magickal bath. It is a well-known fact that taking a bath is synonymous with relaxation. But even more, it is possible to take advantage of this moment to purify ourselves and consciously remove all impurities from our psychic bodies. Through these same baths, we can then begin a reverse process, that is to attract a vibratory energy that will be able to concretize all our desires.

There are two magickal bath techniques. The first consists of a simple *purifying immersion*; a method which you should use abundantly and as often as possible to discharge your psyche; it will do you greater good! The second, rather, serves to imbue and charge your psychic bodies with a specific influence so that it can subsequently manifest concretely, through you, on the earthly plane. This technique is called *magnetic immersion*.

Without further ado, I will explain the two sides of the secret of magickal baths. We will start with the first technique of applying the properties of purifying baths so that you can discharge negative energies. Then we will see, in a second step, how you can charge your subtle bodies with a positive and very constructive influence or vibration.

☆ Purifying Immersions

This type of magickal bath does not require any accessories and is practiced in a short time. You simply need to show a good dose of visualization and your faith as a white witch for the process to really take place, nothing more.

To get rid of the vibrations and negative psychic influences that you will have accumulated over the course of your day, after going out in public or, if you are going to practice a ritual, start by running a bath. Water temperature is irrelevant because this technique does not take into account the magnetic properties of the watery element.

Now place yourself in the bathtub, lie down and focus on the fact that not only do you wash your physical body with soap and water (if you want to wash physically, it will definitely be a good thing), but you will also cleanse and purify your subtle bodies at the same time.

Firmly visualize that anything negative is leaving you at this moment. You can imagine, for example, that your bodies purify themselves by letting all this psychic filth escape into the water through all the pores of your skin. When you are convinced that you have cleansed your whole being in this way, pull the plug and stay in the tub. Visualize that all these unhealthy and discordant energies flow completely with the bathwater into the drain.

When the bathtub is empty, get out and dry yourself. The purifying immersion is completed. It is as simple as that. You can be certain that if you have clearly visualized the rejection of hostile vibrations, the purification was a success. You can then go about your daily activities or put on your magick robe to practice a ritual, knowing you are now discharged from all negative vibratory influences. This technique is easy, fast and very effective.

☆ The Quick Shower

What I call the quick shower is no more or less a variation of purifying immersions. As not everyone has the leisure to own a bathtub or because sometimes time is short and taking a full bath can be somewhat tedious, depending on the circumstances of the moment, it is then possible to purify ourselves quickly under a stream of running water.

The technique is essentially the same as before. In the shower, visualize that all the negative energies absorbed by your psychic bodies escape through all the pores of your skin. Visualize these bad vibrations evacuating and being dragged by the water flowing down your body to your feet. Concentrate intensely on this purifying action for a few minutes. Once this conscious action is complete, get out of the shower and dry yourself. You are now free from all discordant vibrations.

☆ Magnetic Immersions

Unlike the purifying immersions which serve merely to banish hostile and negative vibrations, the following technique, although it can also purify or exorcise discordant vibrations, is used primarily to charge and magnetize the water in the bathtub with a positive and constructive influence or vibration so as to subsequently impregnate your subtle bodies. The first technique *absorbs* vibrations, while the latter *transmits* them.

Those of you who have had the opportunity to study my book of High Magick *La Science des Mages*[2] will notice that I have already clearly demonstrated how magnetic immersions act. However, having adequately explained the magick technique in this book, I will simply repeat here these explanations so you can benefit from them.

If you have ever studied the occult somewhat, you have surely come across a concept of esoteric practices commonly referred as 'magick baths'. For some, if not the majority of the popular mass, taking a magickal bath means running a relaxing, warm and comfortable bath to which

---

2   *La Science des Mages* : Les Immersions Magnétiques p :86 et seq.

you add a handful of herbs or specifically chosen essences. We burn an incense stick, light a few candles and *voilà*. We then take place in the bathtub to enjoy the influences of the said herbs with special properties. If this corresponds roughly to your conception of magickal baths, know that such a ritual bath is no more than to bathe in a huge herbal tea! For such a practice is worthless from the point of view of the experienced magician.

The secret of magick baths lies in the magnetic properties inherent in the aqueous Element. Water, by its nature, has magnetic properties. The hotter the water, the more non-existent the magnetic properties of the water will be. When water reaches the human body temperature of 37 degrees Celsius, its magnetic power then becomes neutralized. Above this temperature, the water is no longer magnetic. This explains why a magick bath in hot water is inoperative, unless of course you know how to charge the water differently by the akashic principle. I will come back to that in a few moments.

On the other hand, the colder the water, the higher its magnetic absorption capacity will be. It will then be easy for the magician to charge this water with a specific desire or quality, just as we saw with the air. Subsequently, by taking a bath in this cold and charged water, it will be sufficient to visualize intensely, always with force and conviction, that the magnetic charge which was impregnated into the water is transmitted through it, to the etheric and psychic body of the magus during this immersion.

Thus, water under its dense physical and material aspect is considered in occultism as a battery accumulator of charges that can be transmitted to the magician. I mentioned to you that it was however possible to use hot water to transmit a given charge to the etheric and astral bodies. Although I recommend you always use the coldest water possible, it is normal to understand that such a bath would quickly cause numbness and discomfort when we are not used to it. Concentration would be equally affected. But after only a few reiterations, you will see it becoming easily bearable.

Also, if you wish to use temperate or even warm enough water, then you must know this water *will not be magnetized*, on the contrary, it will have to be charged directly from the akashic principle (Element of Spirit); the primordial plane of the fifth Element. In this way, the temperature of the water will hardly matter because the charge of the latter will be able to produce and bring the expected effects through the four other Elements under the action of the electromagnetic fluid. However, I will not complicate things further at this stage of your training with even more elaborate explanations in the development of this last technique. Instead, consider the one mentioned above, which is just as effective and much easier to achieve.

As part of your magickal development, I therefore advise you to make use of this secret in cold water, in order to concretize non-selfish desires such as obtaining success in your practices, health, healing, etc. You will therefore be capable, by placing your hands on the surface of the water, combined with a strong visualization, charge an entire bathtub or even just a bowl of water to then soak your whole body or just your hands and imagine the charge of water is immediately transmitted to your subtle bodies to establish itself, and finally, to manifest instantly on the physical plane of matter.

Obviously, the degree of manifestation and the time it will take for a desire to manifest itself will always be in analogy with the nature of the wish, your level of concentration and your strength of visualization, which must be extremely intense — you must never have the slightest doubt in your mind. Remember one of the witches' six powers: faith.

A magnetic immersion alone can constitute a complete magick ritual. But even better, and if you have time, what I recommend you to do is to take this kind of magickal bath as a preliminary, to prepare yourself for a more complete ritual or ceremony which you will then practice in your sanctuary or magick temple.

It is possible and even recommended to use certain mixtures and vegetal compositions in order to enhance the magickal action, but especially vibratory, when taking a ritual bath in warm or cold (read magnetic) water. Although a high level of visualization may be more than sufficient among very experienced practitioners, if you wish to use herbal support (see the chapter dealing with *vegetal compositions for magickal baths and incense*) to add them to your bath or to burn together as incense, you are then encouraged to do so if you desire it, as long as their correspondence has been carefully analyzed before their use. You will understand, however, that these will only be good auxiliaries as long as the key and essential element (water) has been previously charged and magnetized with your will.

As you now know the magick technique for charging water, it will now be easy to effectively practice magnetic immersion rituals or, if you prefer, 'magickal baths'. This concluded the secret regarding magnetic immersions.

$$)O($$

✭ Example of a Magick Bath Ritual

In order to make sure you can properly integrate the practice a ritual magnetic immersion, I will cite you an example of a magick bath. You will only need to follow this procedure for all the baths you will undertake, regardless of the nature or functions they will have to perform, as the process will remain essentially the same.

I will employ the personal form of 'I' so that you can follow me easily, just as if I were preparing myself a magickal bath. I think the example will, this way, be clearer for all.

Suppose I desire to achieve general success in my life. Looking at the correspondences and influences of the Planetary Spheres in the fourth part of this book, I see the Sun seems to be optimal for this kind of ritual.

Having determined that the Solar Cosmic Sphere governs the success I wish to obtain, I know that if I do not employ a real magick lamp, the candles to be used for my ritual bath will have to be golden or, at least, yellow or white. Now, knowing the Sun is in force on Sunday, I will calculate the planetary hours in order to know what is the favorable time of day to work under the power of the Sun, ensuring the coming Sunday will be under an increasing lunar phase to make the most of all the energies conducive to the accomplishment of my magickal action. Once all this is established, I will then choose a plant composition that will serve as incense and a mixture for my magnetic immersion to increase the flow of occult vibrations. Therefore, I just have to wait until the day arrives to practice my ritual magick bath.

So far, what I have checked to perfect my practice of a magickal bath are the following points:

- The Sphere of existence or Planet corresponding to my desire
- The lunar phase
- The planetary day
- The planetary time
- The color of the candles to be used
- The formula of incense and magick bath

In the event that I am unable to calculate the planetary hours, I could always consider practicing my ritual on the Solar day, without worrying about the hour, knowing the Solar Star dominates throughout the day. I also know it would be preferable to operate at the right time, but if I cannot, there is no reason to worry about it.

Sunday having arrived, the time has come to practice my magickal bath. I prepare my bathroom. I place near the bath the golden candles in the shape of a hexagram on a bedside table. I will use six candles because the six-pointed star is a Solar symbol. At the center of the star, I place a white candle to represent myself.

I now place my incense burner nearby, so that I can pour incense from time to time while lying in the bathtub. I will now run the bathwater; a rather cold water because I know that the colder the water, the better its magnetic properties. While my bath fills up, I take the opportunity to turn off the ringtone from the phone making sure I will not be disturbed during the entire ritual. Everything is now ready.

I start by mentally charging my herbal mixture, holding the bottle in my hands. I focus on their Solar properties that will help me achieve success. Then I light the candles and the charcoal pellet in my incense burner. I place a quantity of incense on the embers, as well as in the water of the bathtub.

Now I kneel down and, by laying my hands on the surface of the water, combined with an intense visualization, I charge the bathtub water with my desire for success. After several minutes of deep concentration, I take place in the bath.

The most important part of the ritual has arrived. I visualize very strongly that the charge of water is directly transmitted to my subtle bodies and manifests itself immediately on the physical plane of matter. I have faith in what I do, and I know for a fact that the magnetism of water is transmitted to me through the action of my will. I constantly absorb this magnetic charge and remain concentrated for several minutes while bathing in these Solar vibrations, produced by the action of my visualization, incense, herbs and candles.

When my concentration begins to wane or after about fifteen minutes, the ritual bath is completed. I get out of the tub without drying myself and I let the candles burn completely. I avoid leaving my home while the candles are burning in order to always bathe in these high Solar vibrations, which are still active.

That is how this practice should ideally unfold. By following this example, you will be able to perfect this technique and accomplish all your magickal baths without any difficulty.

THE USE OF LIGHT &
MAGICK LAMPS

Light holds a very privileged, if not essential, place in a consciousness of life harmonized with nature and the forces of the Universe. Light symbolizes what is the purest and highest from a vibratory and spiritual point of view: the Divine.

Moreover, light also plays a significant role in Magick as a vibratory agent and transmitter. The light produced by one or more magick lamps emits an energetic radiation, a specific subtle frequency, which, depending on the color of the light used, generates a particular vibration that will resonate in perfect harmony with given Intelligences and Spheres of existence.

Indeed, the nature of the Entities or Celestial Spheres will be expressed, among other things, by the graduation of the luminous brilliance or, if you prefer, by the color. A white practitioner or magician wanting to work with

Entities from higher Spheres will have to understand that their emanations are very bright and exceedingly shining; they practically irradiate. As a result, the color to be used will be purple, gold or white. On the other hand, the further one moves away from spiritual refinement and approaches the density and the lower Spheres, the more dull, dark and dirty the color of the light, like grey or black.

Generally, the authentic magickal lamp used by mages according to the hermetic precepts consists of a wick soaked in alcohol; an oil lamp covered with tinted glass or cellophane so as to color the brightness of the light produced. This is where the secret of lamps lies. If you do not want to employ such an instrument, do like most modern witches and opt instead for colored candles. However, the effect obtained will not be exactly the same, but let us say it is what will come closest to real magick lamps.

Also, never perform rituals under electric light. The reason why it is strongly discouraged to operate under artificial lighting is that electricity, when it is emitted on the physical plane of matter, blurs and disturbs the astral vibrations which are then fully active during a ritual.

You see now that it is necessary to understand, at first, the action of the light before utilizing it to be able to know exactly what colors will be propitious and analogous to the Cosmic forces and energies that govern certain aspects of the magickal rituals you will practice afterwards. In other words, everything and I mean entirely everything is interrelated, from the plane of matter to the high Celestial Spheres. Remember this. In order for you to avoid mistakes in the choice of the colors of the magick lamps, I have prepared for you at the end of this chapter a section dealing with the occult correspondences of the colors based on the vibrational frequencies of the Universal energies.

✫ Types of Magickal Correspondences Associated with Colors

Before approaching the practical part and using candles in your daily rituals, some explanations are now necessary to correct an erroneous reasoning for too long in circulation. You may indeed be doing this yourself without being fully aware of it. Know there are, so to speak, two ways of determining and associating the colors of the lamps with their magickal correspondences; the good and the bad: the vibrational and those of a psychological order.

It is extremely important you recognize the difference between these methods before going any further. Doing otherwise, you may not obtain all the anticipated results during the practice of your rites due to the fact of having used colors that do not resonate in any way with a precise and well-defined occult action.

✫ The Vibratory Correspondences

The accurate method for analyzing the magickal influences of colors is characterized by the study of vibratory correspondences, which has no other purpose than to scrupulously associate the energetic forces and frequencies that are in sympathy with each other.

To understand the last statement, you must first know that everything that exists in the Universe and the different planes of existence consists of energies. Now, here on earth, the energies we find in nature all vibrate at various levels or frequencies, which are analogous to the vibratory fields generated by certain Celestial bodies. Moreover, *what we find on the scale of the terrestrial plane is only a coarse densification of a much higher, subtle and refined Celestial energies*. In other words, the physical manifestations are only a small, reduced glimpse of what the Universe conceals in all its greatness.

Now take a pause. Take the time to reread what was merely explained if it seems obscure or relatively complicated. If you are still able to follow me, then let us continue together.

Knowing therefore that *what we find on the material plane represents only the dense reflection on a small scale of something much larger and more ethereal*, it is normal that the majority of people have difficulty in interpreting the proper magickal correspondences, because one must possess an open-mindedness that goes beyond the level of the raw matter.

Having demonstrated the vibratory links between the stars and the matter, while being aware that color expresses the nature of Entities and Celestial Spheres, it is completely logical to turn to them in order to determine the exact essence of the magickal correspondences, which will be in perfect analogy with our desires and wishes.

Consequently, the use of colors in Magick must always be based on a thorough study of correspondence. These colors will not constitute ideas or concepts that will be the result of a simple deduction. On the contrary, the purpose of the magick lamps (or the color of the candles) will be to attract and reproduce the same vibratory frequency of a Sphere of existence, which governs a specific terrestrial domain, so that this Cosmic energy can manifest itself inside the magick temple.

By integrating these notions, you will also understand at the same time, why it is just as favorable to align perfectly with the auspicious waves by working on the planetary days and hours. Everything is and will always remain a question of energies and vibratory rate.

✫ Psychological Correspondences

My experience tells me that a considerable majority of books dealing with the correspondence attributed to the colors are rather of a psychological nature. I am even almost convinced, that most practitioners and witches opt for this method of associating the occult powers of colors without knowing exactly that the shades used are not always in precise agreement with the very nature of their rituals.

To illustrate my point, I will cite you the most common example and, at the same time, the mistake made by almost all practitioners who do not bother to think and study their Art conscientiously as it should be before acting.

If I tell you that green is associated with money, you will surely answer me that this is true. Unfortunately, this is not the case. Yet, if you do research, sooner or later you will find in other books or various sources that green is indeed associated with money. So, where does this so popular mistake lie? Indeed, green *psychologically* corresponds to money. However, it does not *vibrationally* correspond to the latter.

Money, commerce and business vibrate essentially with Jupiterian strength and auspices whose color is *blue*. Thus, the correct association would be the use of a light or several blue candles to symbolize money and monetary wealth. Why then do the majority of witches use green? This is quite simple you will see. What color is the American dollar? Yes, it is green! Hence, knowing that a good part of the books of witchcraft come from America, it is normal to understand how this color was quickly associated with money. Though, *psychologically* speaking, in the minds of Occidental authors and practitioners, green symbolizes the so coveted dollar.

This is what psychological associations or correspondences consist of. It is the simple fact of inferring that this or that thing is in perfect analogy with a specific vibration simply because it seems to make sense. Clearly, doing so could compromise the smooth running of a magickal action based on planetary and vibratory influences.

You must probably wonder now if psychological associations are still acceptable in practices of White Magick. Although it is said that what seems good for someone is good for him, it needs be understood first and foremost that Magick summons the natural, Cosmic and Universal energies. In order to attract the proper influences, you must be able to create a channel of vibrations that will be of the same frequency as the goals of your magickal operations. Therefore, you should personally opt without the slightest hesitation, for vibratory and accurate associations, to the detriment of psychological associations, even if it means changing a habit well rooted in your conception for several years.

Of course, I am only your guide. It is up to you to take what you think is appropriate among these pieces of erudition, what seems adequate and put the rest aside. I would simply like to conclude by asking you to take a few moments to meditate on these words and am convinced that in the future, you will choose the right magickal correspondences according to the rules of the Art.

☆ The Use of Candles in Witchcraft

Burning a candle by concentrating with all the power of one's will in order to accomplish an occult action or manifest a specific desire is probably one of the most simplistic rituals that exists in White Magick. This practice has been in use for a long time, and it seems to have not lost its popularity.

Many believe it is preferable to make your own candles so as to mix herbs in the wax to reinforce its magickal power. If you want to make your own candles, I encourage you to do so. Not only will you find pleasure in doing so, but what is more, you will know you will have in your possession a special magickal object which, by the simple fact of having taken your time to design it focusing on its properties, you will be able to obtain more powerful candles than those found in stores. However, you should know this is not necessarily required, as the candles you buy in the supermarket are nevertheless largely sufficient.

Although it is possible to use the candles in a customary way, that is, simply light them without any prior preparation, several witches prefer however to anoint them with essential oils or oil-based occult compositions to charge them with their will and enhance their vibratory effects.

If you choose this technique, which seems to me very fair to do, because in this way you can charge the candles with your personal magnetism, then you have to know how to anoint them. Indeed, it is not enough to simply plunge it in a mixture or rub it with your finger.

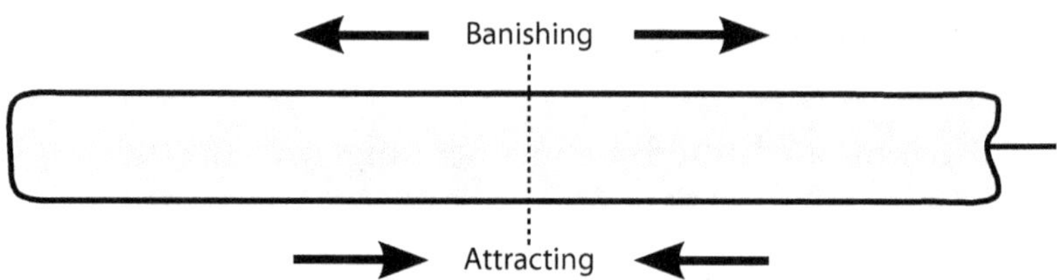

The art of anointing candles with oils

The method used by all white practitioners, when comes the time to apply an oil, is to anoint the index finger of the right hand and go from the center of the candle to the wick, then again from the center to the other extremity, when it is used to *banish* influences. When it comes to *attracting* vibrations, the oil is applied inversely, that is, from the ends towards the center. In conforming to this method, anoint it completely, focusing firmly on the vibrations that the candle should manifest.

Depending on the rituals you perform, sometimes you will need to burn your candles for a specified period of time, such as dividing the candles into seven separate sections so that only one is burned per day, for rituals spanning over a period of seven consecutive days. On the other hand, it will sometimes be asked to let the candles burn out completely so that the magickal action continues, even when the ritual is completed and the magick circle is returned to the Universe. Either way, the use will always be relative to the needs of the rituals in question or rather, depending on what you deem appropriate to do. Light and candles have always been an integral part of Magick and tomorrow is not the day that we will see their use cease.

✫ The True Magickal and Vibratory Correspondences of Colors

One of the best methods to determine what are the correspondences of the most common color, is to consult the planetary auspices that you will find in the fourth part of this book (see the influence of the days of the week). Since we know that all existing things in the Universe are intimately connected to each other, and primarily to the Spheres of existence, from these correspondences, we are therefore able to employ the colors of the candles which will be vibrationally analogous to the aims and desires governed by the planetary Spheres. For example, green for Venus and love, blue for Jupiter and money, red for Mars and courage, etc.

Gold
- The Sun and all Solar correspondences
- The God
- High vibrations, Entities and higher Cosmic Spheres
- Spirituality and the divine
- Healing, protection and purification
- Success and prosperity
- Luck, victory and glory

Silver
- The Moon and all Lunar correspondences
- The Goddess
- Clairvoyance and prophecies
- Psychic powers
- Astral travel and the psyche
- Dreams

White
- Can represent the Sun or the Moon and their correspondences
- High vibrations, Entities and higher Cosmic Spheres
- Spirituality, the divine and peace
- Purity and purification
- Protection and healing

Black and Dark Purple
- Saturn and all Saturnian correspondences (dark purple)
- Banishings, unhexing and exorcisms
- Absorption and return of negative energies
- Destruction of spells and curses
- Necromancy, fatality, death, the deceased
- The astral plane
- Funerals
- End of cycles

Light Purple
- The akashic substance and the Element of Spirit
- High vibrations, Entities and higher Cosmic Spheres
- Spirituality and the elevation of the being
- Wisdom and mastery
- Character ennoblement
- The absolute power of the mage
- Meditation

Orange
- Mercury and all Mercurian correspondences
- Divination and prophecies
- Knowledge and awareness
- Schools, teaching and learning
- Communications
- Movement and travel
- Inspiration and intellectual activity
- Wisdom

Yellow

- Can also represent the Sun and Solar correspondences
- Air Element and its basic correspondences
- Communication and eloquence
- Intellectual faculties
- Creativity, imagination and inspiration
- Persuasion, joy and pleasure
- Application, skill, warmth and optimism

Green

- Venus and all Venus correspondences
- Earth Element and its elementary correspondences
- Love and romantic affairs
- Healing, Remission and Health
- Abundance and fertility
- Esteem, perseverance and depth
- Temperance, punctuality and responsibility
- Female sexuality

Blue

- Jupiter and all Jupiterian correspondences (royal blue)
- Water Element and its elementary correspondences
- Business and money
- Protection
- Patience and wisdom
- Feelings and gentleness
- Modesty, sobriety and fervor
- Compassion, tranquility, calm and forgiveness

Red
- Mars and all Martian correspondences
- Fire Element and its elementary correspondences
- Attack and defense
- Will and passions
- Activity, enthusiasm and resolution
- Strength, vitality and power
- Boldness, courage and temerity
- Virility and male sexuality

Pink
- Friendship, affections
- Platonic relations
- Well-being
- Relaxation

Brown
- Telluric energies
- Stability
- Grounding
- Ability to focus
- Animals
- Wildlife

Gray
- Lower Astral
- Destruction of spells and curses
- Absorption of negativity
- Neutrality

OF THE MAGICKAL USE OF INCENSE & FUMIGATIONS

EVER since Antiquity, incense has been used in all religions and spiritual schools. It was intimately associated with the worship of gods and deities. Moreover, incense was once used to bridge the gap between Heaven and Earth, so as to establish direct contact with this aspect of the supreme divinity. In this regard it was said that the fumigations of incense rising upwards had as function of carrying the prayers to Heaven, places of residence of the deities, gods and goddesses.

Although these practices are still common today, we will instead focus our attention on the use of incense in White Magick whose functions, of a much more elaborate nature, differ from simple adoration and religion.

We could cite for this intent the use of fumigations in High Magick during magickal evocations and operations of necromancy. Incense plays a very important role in these complex practices, which are mainly reserved for experienced practitioners. It is used to obtain material densification of Entities and Spirits, which use the dense particles of incense to form a body or physical envelope allowing them to be seen by the eye of flesh and interact on our plane of existence.

Those who engage in Evocative Magick easily understand that incense is of paramount importance. However, since this book will not deal with this type of Magick, this example will be more than enough to give you a simple overview of the use of fumigations. Indeed, if I had to explain these magickal practices, I could not summarize them in just a few pages. I would have to write an entire book to address the subject adequately. If the time is given to me, maybe I'll do it for you one day.

In the meantime, without straying further from the subject that concerns us, we will now study the properties of incense to which you must become familiar, as these are the ones you will use most frequently during your witchcraft practices.

☆ The Occult Properties of Incense

There are at least two main functions to incense. The primary one consists in intoxicating the operator's consciousness so that it can fall into a second state proper to the accomplishment of a ritual, while the secondary one serves to adjust the vibratory atmosphere so that it is in perfect analogy with a Sphere of existence, thus allowing the latter to manifest itself on the earthly plane.

When I speak of intoxication, you understand, of course, that it is not a question of burning incense abundantly until suffocating! As I have merely mentioned, intoxication means the alteration of consciousness in Magick. That is, incense acts on the mind of the operator in such a way as to raise the level of perception and concentration on a faster, altered and subtle frequency. This daze is sometimes described in terms of trance. When consciousness rises to a higher level, it then becomes possible to align quickly and adequately with occult frequencies or currents. During a ritual, these currents are none other than the energies resonating with an aspect of life, a need, an earthly or Universal matter.

As for the vibratory atmosphere, it is the great magickal secret of incense. To understand this occult property, we must first know that plants, herbs and trees are true receptacles of the Cosmic forces. When we strive to group their specific properties under the same affinity, we obtain herbal compositions of admirable effects.

In the Universe, everything, every number, color, sound and fragrance is unique and holds a very specific vibration. By thus joining vibratory frequencies intimately connected to each other, as in the case of plants and herbs, it is then possible to provoke vibratory effects that will reverberate on the subtle planes as well as on the physical plane of matter. When these vibrations are released from their material envelopes and awakened by the action of fire, by burning a composition of incense, it then becomes possible to align with these emitting waves because they open a channel, allowing here below the manifestation of

Celestial energies proper to a given matter or a specific desire for fulfilment.

However, for a Sphere of existence or a Universal energy, in accordance with an intended purpose, to be able to manifest itself on the terrestrial plane and therefore within the magick circle during rituals, it is necessary to know how to adjust the vibratory rate so that they can radiate or express themselves. Just as a fish that would be removed from water and thus from its natural environment, in order to survive, it would be imperative to recreate an atmosphere corresponding to its sphere of origin, otherwise it could not subsist for long time out of water. Do you follow me? As the fish of this allegory needs water to express itself and to exist, it is necessary to recreate in the magick temple, with the help of incense fumigations (as well as for the light), a vibration identical to a given Sphere so that it can manifest and live there.

It is then that depending on the incense used, the effects on the consciousness and vibratory atmosphere will be just as different. Incense that is very dense and closer to the lower astral nature will have an influence of deceleration, heaviness and numbness on the practitioner who uses it. These fumigations will at the same time facilitate the creation of an environment of low frequencies, allowing the manifestations of the deceased and disembodied as well as of less evolved Spirits, grotesque and of almost even bestial essence. In contrast, incenses of a Solar nature, for example, will accelerate and elevate consciousness and vibratory atmosphere to a much higher degree, also allowing the manifestations of Intelligences belonging to refined Celestial Spheres.

By knowing and now using this very important new information, you will understand that incense is in no way used in Magick to develop a simple pleasant scent. Its implications are far deeper and more technical, as it has just been demonstrated.

☆ Method of preparation of Incenses

There are two types of incense used in Magick : combustibles and non-combustibles. Combustible incenses include all those who do not require a source of heat throughout their combustion. We find for this purpose incense sticks and cones. It is my opinion that the vibratory effects of these are much less powerful, although they hold a favorite place among most witches because of their simplicity of use.

Noncombustible incenses are plant composition made of herbs, oils and resins that require the use of charcoal pellets to be burned. I recommend without hesitation this type of incense for all your magickal practices. In fact, since you will have the opportunity to prepare your own herbal compositions according to your ritual needs, you will also be assured of their quality and freshness, not to mention that you will know exactly what ingredients they contain.

Ideally, your incense mixtures should be prepared on the planetary days and times corresponding to the Sphere that will be active when you burn your magickal incense. For example, on Sunday when the Sun will be in force to craft Solar compositions, on Thursday at the time of Jupiter for Jupiterian incense and so on. Once again, this is not entirely necessary, but highly recommended. At the very least try to work on the planetary day. The more you act according to the energies, at the moment when they are in action, the more your incense compositions will benefit from certain occult powers.

If you wish to respect this magickal precept, then to avoid repeating the whole process frequently and having to wait each time for the right moment to make your incense, I advise you to make good quantities which you will use more than once, and keep it in airtight glass jars. You will then have to store them in a dark place away from the light and this way, your incense will last for a long time.

When preparing your herbal compositions, charge them with your magnetism and the power of your will. Instill in it your desire that they perform such or such magickal functions so that your incense retains these energies. Some will utter repeated incantations, like mantras, throughout this process as they grind the herbs and resins with a pestle and mortar. Others will light candles and mentally pronounce a sentence that indicates the properties that the incense thus fabricated must contain.

Here is a ritual scheme that will be useful, taking into consideration certain important points when preparing magickal incense:

- Verify correspondences for herbs, oils and resins
- Follow the lunar phase
- Follow the planetary day
- Follow the planetary time

- Light a candle of the planetary color analogous to the incense
- Grind herbs and resins with a mortar and pestle
- Focus on the properties and effects of the incense
- Magnetize the plant composition with one's will
- Recite a phrase or mantra expressing the magickal nature of the incense

In brief, it is possible to compose a simple ritual intended only for the preparation of your magick incense. I will only give you this example because you will be able, with a little judgment, to find a way that suits you best to make your own incense and charge them properly. My only recommendation: when making your herbal incense mixtures, always work consciously. Be focused on what you are doing and visualize that you are powerfully transmitting your energy to the herbs and resins so that they are imbued with your will and vibrations.

☆ Basic Incenses ☆

What we refer to as basic incenses in Magick are mainly natural resins that have been used since time immemorial for their proven superior vibratory effects. They all possess admirable magickal properties, including purification and protection. Based on their correspondence, these resins can be added to all the herbal formulas found in the section dealing with plant compositions for magick baths and incense. Burned on their own, they are remarkable and powerful magickal agents. When used in conjunction with herbal formulas, they will increase the vibratory effects of the latter tenfold. This is inevitable, basic incenses will definitely become your personal favorites when it comes to magickal fumigations.

Here is a list of the most commonly used incenses in Magick:

Arabian incense

This incense is very similar to frankincense. The scent of this resin precipitates the arrival of the Elementals Spirits, who will respond promptly to the action of this incense.

Benzoin

Of Mercurian nature, the benzoin promotes, through the vibrations of its fumigations, commercial prosperity and intellectual activities. In addition, it increases mental inspiration and ideas as well as freedom in professional activities. Combined with pontifical incense, this mixture becomes an excellent agent to carry out the magickal evocations of the 72 genies of the Kabbalah, also known as Mercurian Intelligences.

Camphor

Camphor is lunar in nature. It promotes the purification of the psyche and, as a purifying agent, it provides the cleansing of any places by enhancing the vibratory atmosphere. Camphor crystals are therefore excellent for restoring the psyche and healing, in addition to being all indicated during exorcisms.

Copal

Copal resin is a purifying and protective agent. It brings positive vibrations and helps to center. It therefore also promotes meditation. This incense has been burned for hundreds of years to help and guide the Spirits to find their way home.

Dragon's Blood

Dragon's blood has become an extremely popular resin in Magick. Its fragrance is very strong and pronounced. This incense is used primarily as an antiseptic agent, to purify, banish negative influences, reverse spells, to exorcise and provide protection. This red resin is widely used in Draconic Magick.

Frankincense

The most popular of all incense, frankincense resin, also known as pure incense, is of Solar essence. It is a very great purifying agent. It is used almost everywhere and in all incense compositions and formulas. Frankincense generates very high vibrations, hence giving the user the opportunity to resonate with the highest Spheres. In addition, this basic incense is favorable for evolution, worship, dedicatory acts, protection and exorcisms. It is excellent for all types of rituals.

Incense of Nazareth

This incense vibrates in accordance with the Jupiterian Sphere. Being of a magnetic nature, it will be favorably used to attract vibrations that affect money and financial prosperity, job searches, social elevation, business and legal causes.

Jerusalem incense

The incense of Jerusalem is associated with the Saturnian Sphere. Its purifying fumigations exude the aura and the vibratory atmosphere in such a way as to grant grace and remission of human impurities.

Lourdes incense

This incense acts mainly and with great efficiency on feminine vibrations. Its nature being magnetic, it recharges the magnetism that is related to electric waves and, as a result, restores the electromagnetic deficiencies of the person who uses it. This incense will be essentially beneficial for female practitioners.

Manne

Manne puts us in contact with the Spirits of the Earth. It thus promotes in a remarkable, if not to say astounding way, prosperity and material gains, whether in terms of material goods or money.

Mastic

Mastic resin, also known as lentiscus gum, is usually mixed with other resins and herbal compositions to facilitate psychic powers and visions.

Myrrh

Myrrh resin is associated with the Solar Sphere. It purifies and exorcises, promotes concentration, meditation and spirituality. This basic incense is excellent for all types of rituals because the vibrations generated by the myrrh fumigations considerably increase the vibratory atmosphere.

Pontifical

This incense purifies, protects, but even more, transmutes the surrounding vibrations at an extraordinary speed. That is why it is so excellent for all rituals. Add pontifical incense to herbal incense compositions to enhance remarkably all their magickal effects.

Three Kings

Three Kings resin is of Venusian fiery nature. This incense is excellent for purifying and dispelling harmful and evil influences, is used for rituals of return of affection, helps to resolve sentimental problems, promotes encounters and bonds both in love and friendship and provides harmony.

✮ **Sabbatical Incense Recipes** ✮

The following sabbatical incense compositions have been designed and elaborated to properly charge the vibratory atmosphere of the magickal temple at the time of the rituals, when the occasion comes to celebrate the eight witches' festivals, the Sabbaths. Use these compositions on your sabbatical feasts to honor the God and the Goddess during the different cycles of the wheel of the year.

Samhain
3 — Frankincense
2 — Myrrh
1 — Cedar
1 — Juniper
1 — Rosemary

Yule
2 — Frankincense
2 — Myrrh
2 — Pine
1 — Cedar
1 — Juniper

Imbolg
3 — Frankincense
2 — Dragon's blood
1 — Cinnamon
½ — Red sandalwood
Drops of red wine

Ostara
2 — Frankincense
1 — Benzoin
1 — Dragon's Blood
½ — Nutmeg
½ — Orange
½ — Rose
½ — Violet

Beltane
3 — Frankincense
2 — Sandalwood
1 — Rose
1 — Woodruff
Jasmine oil drops
Orange oil drops

Litha
3 — Frankincense
2 — Benzoin
1 — Dragon's Blood
1 — Rosemary
1 — Thyme
1 — Vervain
Drops of red wine

Lughnasadh
2 — Frankincense
1 — Heather
1 — Blackberry leaves
1 — Apple blossoms
Drops of ambergris oil

Mabon
2 — Frankincense
1 — Cypress
1 — Juniper
1 — Pine
1 — Sandalwood
1 — Oak

)O(

PLANT COMPOSITIONS FOR MAGICK BATHS AND INCENSE

URING your practices of witchcraft and for all your ritual needs, whether it be magick baths (magnetic immersions) or incense fumigations, you can use for these purposes, the special formulas included in this chapter.

I have designed for your attention the following herbal compositions.[3] They have been elaborated meticulously and with great care, in the purest respect of the tradition of magickal correspondences in order to offer you the best of the properties inherent in the plants and herbs that Mother Earth has so wonderfully gifted us.

Know that these recipes provide exactly the same effects and generate the same vibrations, no matter how you employ them. Indeed, these compositions can just as well

---

3   When no quantities are given, all parts are equal.

be used as incense that you will burn in your censer or as a mixture that you will incorporate into the water of your bathtub during your rites of immersions. Better still, it is even recommended to apply both methods simultaneously during magickal baths.

Finally, remember it is also possible, and I encourage you to do so, to add a resin to the formulas presented here, when they are used in fumigations. The reason why I did not specify the type of resin in each recipe is that it is unnecessary to use it for magickal baths. You will easily understand that resins cannot dissolve in water. Refer to the section dealing with basic incense and choose the resins that you see the most appropriate if you want to use them.

☆ **Purification and Exorcism** ☆

The following compositions will prove very effective during rituals for all the needs of purification, unhexing and exorcism; to cleanse and banish the negative influences of the psychic bodies, the mind and the immediate surroundings of the operator.

Formula #1
- Camphor
- Citrus
- Fumitory
- Iris
- Salt

Purification, sanitation, unhexing and exorcism.

Formula #2
- Celery
- Clover
- Cypress
- Fumitory
- Salt

Purification, exorcism, unhexing, keeps away painful trials.

Formula #3
- Anise
- Basil
- Iris
- Rose
- Salt

- Sandalwood

Purifies admirably well and raises the vibratory rate by the action of very beneficial influences.

Formula #4
- Basil
- Matricaria
- Rose
- Salt
- Sandalwood
- Wormwood

Destroys and exorcises larvae, raises the vibratory rate by very positive influences.

Formula #5
- Basil
- Lily
- Salt
- Wormwood
- Yarrow

Destroys larvae, purification, exorcism and unhexing.

Formula #6
- Citrus
- Iris
- Lady's Mantle
- Lavender
- Lemon balm
- Salt

Restores the disturbed psyche and cast away anxieties, purification and sanitation.

Formula #7

* Frankincense
* Basil
* Rose
* Salt

Increases exceptionally the vibratory rate. Brings extremely beneficial influences and vibrations. Very great purifying agent.

☆ **Protection** ☆

The following formulas will be used during rituals for all protection needs, whatever they may be. They will protect the operator at all levels by manifesting very high beneficial vibrations.

Formula #1
- Cedar
- Eucalyptus
- Mistletoe
- Oak
- Pine
- Salt

Excellent all-purpose protection formula!

Formula #2
- Acacia
- Boxwood
- Hyssop
- Laurel
- Salt
- Wormwood

Provides very great protection and chases away fears.

Formula #3
- Boxwood
- Laurel
- Oak
- Orange root

- Pine
- Rosemary
- Salt

Provides very high protection and attracts extremely positive vibrations.

Formula #4

- Eucalyptus
- Juniper
- Oats
- Salt
- Sandalwood

Provides protection and cleansing.

Formula #5

- Basil
- Cedar
- Chamomile
- Chicory
- Mistletoe
- Salt

Provides protection through beneficial vibrations and wards off enemies.

Formula #6

- Basil
- Mustard
- Rose
- Rosemary
- Sage

- Salt

Excellent protection formula that keeps enemies away from the operator.

Formula #7

- Acacia
- Basil
- Orange root
- Rose
- Salt

Protects and increases the vibratory rate and creates extremely beneficial vibrations.

Formula #8

- Citrus
- Lavender
- Marjoram
- Raspberry leaf
- Salt
- Strawberry tree

Provides great protection of the psyche and home.

☆ **Psychism and Psychic Powers** ☆

The following herbal compositions are excellent and highly effective during rituals for all causes involving the development of psychic powers, the faculty of intuition and clairvoyance.

Formula #1
- Acacia
- Basil
- Eyebright
- Flax
- Hyssop
- Mugwort

Best formula helping the development of pure clairvoyance and the acquisition of high psychic faculties.

Formula #2
- Anise
- Basil
- Marshmallow root
- Lily
- Shepherd's purse

Effectively develops psychic faculties and receptivity.

Formula #3
- Angelica
- Anise
- Basil
- Eyebright

- Flax
- Tea tree

Promotes mental activity and the development of high clairvoyance.

Formula #4

- Acacia
- Hyssop
- Mugwort
- Poplar

Illuminates the mind and inspiration and facilitates clairvoyance.

Formula #5

- Birdsfoot trefoil
- Iris
- Lavender
- Marshmallow root
- Shepherd's purse

Develops psychic faculties and helps clairvoyance.

Formula #6

- Basil
- Cedar
- Hyssop
- Laurel
- Mugwort

Formula helping inspiration and the development of high clairvoyance.

Formula #7

- Anise
- Marjoram
- Marshmallow root
- Shepherd's purse
- Willow

Lunar formula helping receptivity, perceptions and divination. Soothes and opens the mind.

☆ **Money and Wealth** ☆

The following compositions will be used for all rituals serving to attract influences and vibrations of a monetary order, money and wealth as well as financial prosperity.

Formula #1
- Bitter dock
- Couchgrass
- Maple
- Sarsaparilla

Jupiterian formula attracting the vibrations of money and wealth.

Formula #2
- Mistletoe
- Orange root
- Saffron
- Sage
- Thyme

Solar formula attracting very positive vibrations favoring money and financial prosperity.

Formula #3
- Bergamot
- Bitter dock
- Couchgrass
- Dandelion
- Fennel
- Lily of the Valley
- Maple

- Rue
- Sarsaparilla

Very complete composition favoring money, earnings and wealth on the material level.

Formula #4
- Basil
- Blessed thistle
- Nettle
- Saffron
- Thyme

Stimulates monetary abundance and protects against money leakage.

Formula #5
- Ash
- Basil
- Ginkgo
- Ginseng
- Matricaria
- Oak

Brings very beneficial influences and attracts money and material wealth.

Formula #6
- Bergamot
- Dandelion
- Fennel
- Lily of the Valley
- Pistachio tree

Provides luck on the material level and attracts money.

Formula #7
- Gingko
- Matricaria
- Mistletoe
- Orange root
- Thyme

Provides beneficial influences favoring the inflow of money.

☆ **Work and Social Elevation** ☆

The use of the following incense and magickal baths recipes will allow the operator to attract and manifest the vibrations conducive to all magickal work related to employment, work relations and personal elevation on a social level.

Formula #1
- Bitter dock
- Couchgrass
- Fern
- Honeysuckle
- Hyacinth
- Laurel
- Mistletoe
- Saffron

Provides beneficial vibrations helping the operator to find work or improve an already established situation.

Formula #2
- Basil
- Birch
- Cloves
- Geranium
- Licorice

Promotes human relations, soothes relational conflicts and provides sincere and elevated feelings.

Formula #3

- Clover
- Orange root
- Saffron
- Sage
- Solomon's seal

Provides stability, success and keeps painful trials away.

Formula #4

- Chicory
- Fern
- Gorse
- Laurel
- Mistletoe
- Mustard
- Saffron

Drives away competition and brings glory and fame to work and social relationships.

Formula #5

- Bitter dock
- Dandelion
- Fern
- Honeysuckle
- Maple
- Pistachio tree
- Saffron
- Sage

Brings very beneficial vibrations favoring employment or improving an already established situation. Also provides luck on a material level.

Formula #6

- Basil
- Couchgrass
- Fern
- Honeysuckle
- Maple
- Mountain ash
- Orange root

Generates very beneficial vibrations favoring all facets pertaining to work and social relationships.

☆ **Love and Feelings** ☆

The occult compositions in this section will be very useful during magickal practices related to love and romantic causes; whether it is a question of breaking chronic loneliness, of arousing desire, burning passions and feelings, or to break a harmful bond or spell, these formulas will satisfy the majority of love needs.

Formula #1
- Damiana
- Jasmine
- Orchid
- Primrose
- Tarragon
- Vanilla
- Violet

Formula to be used by female practitioners in order to arouse sensual desire in men.

Formula #2
- Cumin
- Ginger
- Pine
- Primrose
- Vanilla
- Vetiver

Formula to be used by male practitioners in order to arouse sensual desire in women.

Formula #3

- Basil
- Cinnamon
- Cloves
- Rose

Promotes good understanding, soothes and dissolves relational and emotional conflicts.

Formula #4

- Apricot tree
- Columbine
- Dill
- Vanilla
- Violet

Magnetizes the operator's aura in order to provoke sexual attraction and ignite desires.

Formula #5

- Cinnamon
- Dill
- Gardenia
- Jasmine
- Rose
- Violet

Excellent attraction formula. Attracts love, eroticism and love passions.

Formula #6
- Damiana
- Orchid
- Primrose
- Scabiosa
- Tarragon
- Violet

Ignite passions and attract love and affection from the opposite sex.

Formula #7
- Damiana
- Dill
- Orchid
- Primrose
- Violet

This composition helps to provoke passions and stimulate sensual and erotic desires.

Formula #8
- Apricot tree
- Columbine
- Dill
- Orchid
- Primrose
- Scabiosa
- Vanilla

This composition helps to provoke passions and stimulate sensual and erotic desires.

Formula #9

- Cinnamon
- Damiana
- Elderberry
- Mistletoe
- Orange root
- Primrose
- Rose
- Sandalwood
- Violet

Ideal composition used to promote and provoke a return of affection, of course if the cause is just and without forcing others.

Formula #10

- Birch
- Damiana
- Jasmine
- Orange root
- Primrose
- Rose
- Tarragon
- Violet
- Yarrow

This composition has excellent vibratory effects to counter chronic loneliness and lack of affection.

Formula #11

- Acacia
- Anemone
- Angelica
- Basil
- Chicory
- Oregano
- Potentilla

Composition of choice for unhexing and breaking a harmful bond, a disturbing love or a love that is the fruit of a magickal spell.

☆ **Health, Peace and Well-Being** ☆

The following compositions have been developed to meet the majority of health, peace and well-being needs. To restore the clarity of the psyche, thought and physical vitality, to bring calm, relaxation and healing, to counter depression and melancholy, fatigue, the absence of joie de vivre, as well as to help the dying and the deceased, everything is there.

Formula #1
- Anise
- Cabbage
- Camphor
- Lavender
- Linden
- Strawberry tree

This formula generates very beneficial vibrations in order to calm, soothe and restore the psyche, while purifying the operator very adequately.

Formula #2
- Angelica
- Boxwood
- Laurel
- Mistletoe
- Saffron
- Valerian

This composition is an excellent tonic for the body and mind. Revitalizes the whole being and helps dissolve any form of depression.

Formula #3
- Amaranth
- Beech
- Clover
- Cypress

Very special formula to help the dying and the deceased. Also calls for the remission of karmic debts and keeps harsh trials away.

Formula #4
- Acacia
- Angelica
- Basil
- Cedar
- Chamomile
- Eucalyptus
- Orange root

This composition generates excellent vibrations for healing and health.

Formula #5
- Basil
- Eucalyptus
- Flax
- Laurel
- Mistletoe
- Saffron
- Sage
- St. John's wort

This composition generates excellent vibrations for healing and health.

Formula #6

- Angelica
- Apple tree
- Cedar
- Chamomile
- Laurel
- Mistletoe
- Sesame
- St. John's wort
- Thyme
- Valerian

This composition generates excellent vibrations for healing, health and also dissolves depressive states.

Formula #7

- Eucalyptus
- Laurel
- Mistletoe
- Sandalwood
- Savory
- St. John's wort

Solar formula with beneficial influences bringing good health and longevity.

Formula #8

- Anise
- Citrus
- Lady's Mantle
- Lavender
- Marjoram

- Strawberry tree

Brings relaxation and calms anxieties.

Formula #9

- Angelica
- Apple tree
- Eucalyptus
- Rosemary
- Saffron
- Sandalwood
- Valerian

Brings comfort and harmony. Brings a state of calm and beneficial peace.

Formula #10

- Camphor
- Iris
- Mallow
- Marjoram
- Pansy

Provides a sense of detachment and peace. Purifies thoughts and promotes relaxation.

Formula #11

- Angelica
- Basil
- Cedar
- Eucalyptus
- Marigold
- Rose

- Sandalwood
- Valerian

Brings complete calm, regenerative peace and harmony.

Formula #12

- Bitter dock
- Camellia
- Linden
- Matricaria
- Orange root
- Rose
- Rosemary

Very adequate composition to counter pessimism and melancholy. Provides comfort and restores the joy of living.

☆ **Strength and Power** ☆

The following compositions all have the same particularity. Their essences are only in accordance with the vibrations of the planet Mars. Martian influences have been tested for a long time for all causes involving force, power, courage, attack, defense as well as male virility. However, be careful when using these mixtures because they develop very strong vibratory currents.

Formula #1
- Chili pepper
- Coriander
- Cumin
- Ginger
- Pepper tree
- Pine
- Vetiver

Martian formula whose vibrations generate power, strength and courage in the person who uses it. Also stimulates male virility.

Formula #2
- Chicory
- Coriander
- Cumin
- Dragon's blood
- Garlic
- Ginger

This Martian formula of defense provides power in

combat and against any adversity, regardless of the nature of the latter. If there is one or more opponents, then this formula will be ideal to obtain victory.

Formula #3
- Cinquefoil
- Coriander
- Cumin
- Ginger
- Nettle
- Pine

Martian formula favoring fortitude, strength, courage and power in battle and against adversity.

Formula #4
- Blessed thistle
- Carob
- Chili pepper
- Dragon's blood
- Nettle
- Pine

Martian formula whose vibrations generate power, strength and courage in the person who uses it.

Formula #5
- Chicory
- Mustard
- Nettle
- Pepper tree
- Pine

Martian formula of choice for defense in order to forcefully ward off all enemies of the operator who will use this blend.

Formula #6
- Agave
- Dill
- Ginger
- Ginseng
- Pine
- Vetiver

Fire formula whose uses greatly enhance sexual potency and virility.

Formula #7
- Chili tree
- Dill
- Ginger
- Ginseng
- Pepper tree
- Pine
- Vetiver

Essentially a Martian formula (except for the dill) whose vibrations generate power, strength and courage in the person who uses it. Also stimulates male virility.

☆ **Prosperity, Luck and Success** ☆

As part of your magickal practices, if you want to obtain the manifestation and realization of your projects and occult works, this section dedicated to prosperity, luck and success will be extremely useful to you. The vibrations generated by these formulas will bring success on many levels by countering obstacles, bad luck and trials.

Formula #1
- Basil
- Fern
- Matricaria
- Orange root
- Pineapple
- Saffron
- Sage

This composition generates excellent vibrations bringing luck, glory and fame to all levels.

Formula #2
- Acacia
- Angelica
- Basil
- Boxwood
- Pineapple
- Rose

This composition is ideal to bring splendor to the person for whom it will be used.

Formula #3
- Ash
- Fern
- Ginkgo
- Ginseng
- Oak

This formula brings prosperity and success at all levels and above all, material prosperity.

Formula #4
- Basil
- Bitter dock
- Fern
- Hyssop
- Mistletoe
- Saffron
- Sarsaparilla

Generates excellent vibrations conducive to success and prosperity.

Formula #5
- Apple tree
- Hyssop
- Juniper
- Linen
- Orange root
- St. John's wort
- Tea tree

Excellent formula to attract and promotes luck.

Formula #6
- Juniper
- Laurel
- Saffron
- Sage
- Savory
- St. John's wort

Excellent formula to attract and promote luck.

Formula #7
- Apple tree
- Dandelion
- Laurel
- Mistletoe
- Oregano
- Pistachio tree
- Sage

The vibrations generated by this composition attract luck on the material plane.

FOURTH PART

Harmonizing with Cycles, Time & Cosmos

DAYS OF POWER, LUNAR CYCLES & SEASONS

THE practitioners of the Art are conscious beings who know how to harmonize with the various facets of nature and Universal energies. By doing so, they are capable to recognize the influences and virtues of certain favorable times of the year, in addition to the life cycles to be observed, in order to recharge their batteries, practice Magick more effectively and aspire to new currents produced by occult tides. These opportune moments are characterized as follows:

- Lunar phases
- The daily influence of planets called planetary days and hours
- Sabbaths, including solstices and equinoxes

These periods are mainly marked by the movement of

the stars and planets, but especially by the solar and lunar cycles from which the practitioners find the various attributions of the God and the Goddess, the Father and Mother of all witches.

You will learn within this chapter to harmonize with the celestial cycles and seasons, as well as discover the lunar correspondences and planetary auspices for all the days and hours of the week. By assimilating all this new knowledge, you will also be able to align yourself with the energetic waves and currents corresponding to the very nature of your magick, that is, by knowing when to work, you will succeed in coming into intimate contact with influences and vibrations expressing the same qualities as your desires when taking action during your magickal practices.

Therefore, by acting especially at the right moments, by following the lunar cycle and planetary influences, you will know which are the most favorable periods to practice your rituals in order to bathe in the energy capable of manifesting and concreting all your magickal acts of witchcraft. You will hence put all the chances on your side. It is like saying that working at the right times is the same as moving in the same direction of the wind, whereas working in the wrong occult periods would be like rowing against the current; you will probably manage to reach the other shore, but it will be oh how much more difficult! As you can see, witches consistently act meticulously by applying all the rules of their knowledge.

☆ Lunar Phases and Cycles

The moon, like the sun, is one of the oldest natural calendars on earth. We find many evidences of this attraction for the lunar star within various cultures and religions all around the world as well as in several myths and legends. Furthermore, crescent moons are also the sacred symbols of the Goddess in addition of being symbolic of Magick, fertility and the occult powers of nature. In brief, the power of the moon has been implored, but above all, duly experienced by the peoples of the Earth since the dawn of time because of the energetic power it has so admirably demonstrated over the past many centuries.

In order to bathe in the favorable energies tending towards the accomplishment of all your magickal practices, the first consideration to take will always be the lunar phase. The moon and its cycles affect many aspects of our lives, as much in human beings, as in animals and nature, and the same applies to Magick.

Knowing the lunar star creates occult tides which are also referred to as fluctuations at the level of psychic energy fields, it is therefore obvious that these currents will have a direct influence on all creation and, of course, on the energies deployed and manifested during magickal rituals or ceremonies.

In witchcraft practices, the lunar phases always prove to be excellent indicators of what your magick should be or, again, to what intent your magickal acts should be directed. Now, remember that there are exactly thirteen complete lunar cycles per year, or thirteen full moons at the rate of one per month. However, there will be one moth per year that will have two full moons, the thirteenth one called *blue moon*.

Now, on a more practical side, we will first look at what are all the cyclical periods or lunar phases to observe. Although we can count several different periods and influences in the course of this star around the Earth, eight, to be more precise, we will however in a second place, narrow our field of vision to the most important phases to effectively practice White Magick.

The different lunar phases are as follows:

1. New Moon or Black Moon
2. Waxing Crescent
3. First Quarter
4. Waxing Gibbous
5. Full Moon
6. Waning Gibbous
7. Last Quarter
8. Waning Crescent

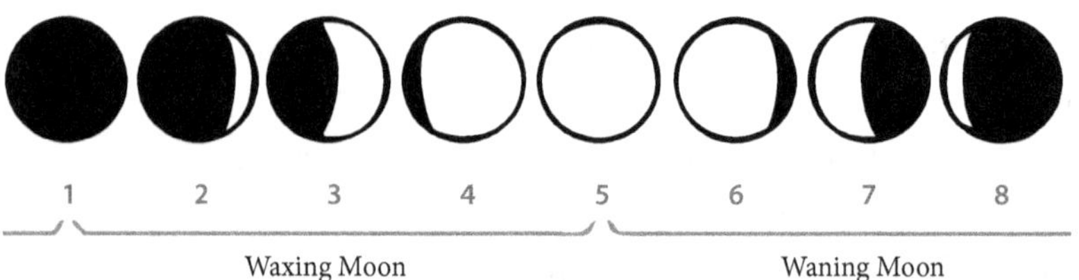

Lunar phases

New Moon or Black Moon

This lunar phase has two distinct functions. First, the new moon or black moon marks both the end of the lunar cycle, as well as its perpetual renewal. It is the axis on which the culmination, conclusion and renewal or rebirth of the lunar cycle overlap. On one hand, the black moon symbolizes the ideal time to sow new ideas; it is the proper moment to give birth to new projects or to start a long-term ritual that will be spread over the duration of the lunar growth.

On the other hand, the black moon, seen as the conclusion of the lunar cycle, still has part of its negative aspect. This is the perfect time for witches and evil practitioners to give free rein to their harmful and morally questionable practices and hexes. In any case, as far as you are concerned, consistently work for the good and aspire only to noble goals.

Waxing Crescent

The waxing crescent represents the time to concretely prepare the ground of fertility, the time to implement the ideas and projects that germinated during the new moon. We subsequently begin attracting to ourselves all that is of a positive nature, whether materially, emotionally or spiritually. This is the time to take action and set in motion all the works of light and to practice all the rituals of beneficial and constructive Magick.

First Quarter

The first quarter, as for the waxing crescent, is always

a beneficial moment to attract positive influences towards oneself. This period, which is halfway between the new and the full moon, is the extension and continuity of the crescent lunar phase.

Waxing Gibbous Moon

The influences of the full moon are already beginning to be felt; the last moment of the lunation is rapidly approaching. The energy emitted by the lunar star becomes more and more intense. It is generally said that the influences of the full moon begin three days before it reaches its full growth, from the waxing gibbous moon and extends three days thereafter to the waning gibbous moon. This phase is a constructive and very positive moment that conceals a strong energy power.

The Full Moon

The full moon is the culmination of all lunations. It is the precise moment when the lunar energy reaches its peak. The energetic influence is at its highest level of intensity; it is a time of ultimate and privileged power for all beneficial and constructive magick rituals. It is not difficult to understand why the moon in full growth represents every witch's favorite moment. The full moon also means the time has come to harvest, for all that has been ritually sown during the growing phase will now have to be completed.

Waning Gibbous Moon

Although the moon has now begun its decline cycle, the waning gibbous moon still benefits from the strong influences of the passed full moon. Latecomers will be able to work under this lunar phase as if it were the full moon itself, but without abusing it. Indeed, as it is the time of decrease, magickal practices should instead now be oriented so as to banish all unwanted, negative or destructive influences from ourselves.

Last Quarter

The last quarter is always a good time to repel and exorcise negative energies at all levels. This period halfway between the full and the new moon is the extension and continuity of the decreasing lunar phase.

Waning Crescent

Now is the time to finalize the acts of exorcism and banishment. The black moon quickly approaching, indicates that all magickal works used to drive away destructive and negative energies are also coming to an end.

As we can see, some lunar phases are very similar due to the resemblance of their energetic effects. It is not essential to recall all these cycles because the most important lunar phases to remember can be summarized as follows:

- New moon
- Waxing moon (*waxing crescent, first quarter and waxing gibbous moon*)
- Full moon
- Waning moon (*waning gibbous moon, last quarter and waning crescent*)

From these four references only, you will be capable to effectively practice all your magick rituals and rites, charms and spells. Generally speaking, we could say, as a complement to the previous explanations, that the new moon will mark the end of one cycle and the beginning of another: death and birth. As for the full moon, the culminating point in terms of psychic energies, it is the ideal moment to achieve fulfillment and work in force in any field, whatever it may be.

Finally, during the waxing moon, your magickal initiatives will follow the same movement and *grow*. The crescent lunar period or the moon of light possesses a force of attraction which we could determine by *magnetic effects*; that is, just like a magnet, it is the opportune time to attract to you all that is of a beneficial nature, whether it is about financial, romantic, personal, spiritual causes, briefly, everything that has a positive character.

In contrast, during a waning moon or shadow moon, this period qualifies in terms of *repellent effects*. Like the other pole of the magnet, you will take advantage of this time to exorcise, chase away and divest yourself of negative and hostile influences or, if you prefer, get rid of what bothers you. For example, banishing negative energies at home or at work, driving away dark thoughts and unhealthy intentions as well as bad habits. In other words, anything that possesses a negative character.

In conclusion, you will see that working closely with the lunar phases will increase the power of your rituals tenfold. I am not saying it is obligatory to abide by these cycles, not to mention counting the planetary days and hours, which the explanations will follow immediately afterwards, but if you wish to obtain the best from your magickal actions, most likely you will pay attention to these essential notions in order to act under the influence of the most favorable energetic currents.

)○(

☆ The Influences and Correspondences of the Planetary Spheres

The planets influence in turn every moment of the week as well as each hour of the day. They thus subtly pour on Earth a flood of energies that affect us all in various areas, without us realizing it. However, those who know the secrets of Magick are aware of the nature of the vibrations caused by these celestial bodies and they will apply them daily in rites and ceremonies in order to enhance their effects. In all, we count seven main planets; each associated with a calendar day. From Sunday to Saturday, they respectively are the Sun, the Moon, Mars, Mercury, Jupiter, Venus and Saturn.

For a very long time, the ancients, whether they are occultists, magicians, Kabbalists or witches, have noticed and attributed multiple correspondences and properties to the planets. Each has influences and auspices that you can use to increase the power of your rituals. These same ancients stipulate that *everything wants to be done under its own planet,* and this is exactly what I recommend you do if you aspire to achieve the best possible results.

By practicing a ritual on the planetary day and time corresponding to the nature of your magickal action, you will put all the chances on your side to achieve your ends. Tell yourself that when doing something, you might as well do it right. Let us cite as examples that love charms should therefore be practiced in the day and hour of Venus, while those in need for protection can act when Mars is in force, as well as on Thursday regarding financial causes, etc.

Here are now the planetary influences, vibrations and auspices for the seven days of the week. From these correspondences, it will be easy for you to determine when you should practice your rituals so as to align with the energies analogous to your desires. Remember that the more you do so, the better your hopes of success will be.

Sun — Sunday

Solar auspices are conducive to health, healing, protection, spirituality, attaining glory and honor, luck, success, harmony, peace, personal confidence, friendships, the prevention of disputes and wars, eternal youth, enlightenment, the Divine power.

Moon — Monday

Lunar auspices are conducive to female fertility, receptivity and prophecy, dreams, sleep, healing, fertility in general, agriculture, the sea, natural medicines, changes, births, skills, home and family, prevent wars, reconciliations, psychism and psychic powers.

Mars — Tuesday

♂

Martian auspices are conducive to attack and defense, aggression, war and conflict, sexual desire, sensual and sexual force in man, courage, physical strength, power, protective guard, breaking spells, prison, weapons, military matters, debates, competition and domination.

Mercury — Wednesday

☿

Mercurian auspices are conducive to divination, predictions, mental powers, thought, intellect, influencing others, wisdom, learning and gaining knowledge, inspiration, awareness, communications, travel, movement, schools, teaching, studies, commercial successes and clientele, exams, writing and authors.

Jupiter — Thursday

♃

Jupiterian auspices are conducive to monetary causes, finance and money, prosperity, luck and good fortune or poverty, gambling, leadership, legal matters, materialism, social elevation, employment, trade, wealth, abundance, career success and ambitions.

Venus — Friday

♀

Venusian auspices are conducive to love causes, romance, affections, relationships, friendship, beauty, fidelity, pleasures and youth, artistic activities and arts, music, parties and lust, close friendships, aphrodisiacs, sexual desire, sensuality and sexual strength in women.

Saturn — Saturday

♄

Saturnian auspices are conducive to necromancy, karma, reincarnation, countering and repelling negative vibrations, science, change, politics, responsibilities, debts, acquiring the astral plane, death, funerals, the end of cycles, exorcisms and purification, disenchantments, breaking spells and psychic attacks, obtaining esoteric secrets.

☆ Calculation of Planetary Hours

Knowing it is possible to multiply the power of your rituals by working when the planets analogous to your desires will be in force, you will additionally have to determine how to calculate the planetary hours in order to make the most of these magickal influences.

If you work only under the planet of the day, it is already great, but if you combine this the time at which this same planet will be dominant, even better will be the effects obtained. Indeed, you now know the planets dominate in turn one day of the week but, even more, during the same day, these planets will take turns and rotate every hour of the day. This is why it is important to understand how to calculate the planetary hours.

Every day, the planets rule a few hours of the daylight as well as certain hours of the night. You must understand that the hours of a planetary day are not calculated according to our clocks. In fact, daytime hours are calculated according to the duration of sunlight and nights, according to the period of darkness. You will evidently understand from these explanations that the planetary days, during the winter, will therefore be considerably shorter than during the summer.

A planetary day will always consist of 12 hours of day and 12 hours of night. However, you must start by determining what is the number of hours of sunlight in a given day. By finding those number of hours, you will inevitably obtain the night hours as well.

As I know some of you will be thinking, '*Hey! Wait a minute. I don't understand!*' I will consequently provide to you an example to clarify everything so that you can follow me in my explanations. You will see, it is much less complicated than it may seem.

Let's say, for example, that today the sun rose at 6:00 in the morning and it will set at 9:00 pm. The total duration of sunlight will determine the hours of the day. Here, the period of the day will be 15 hours. Now, knowing that the planetary days are all 12 hours of day and 12 hours of night, we will divide the number of hours of sunlight by 12 to determine the length of each hour of the planetary day. Though, 15 hours of sunlight are equivalent to 900 minutes, so divided by 12 gives us a total of 75 minutes. Here, today's planetary hours will last 75 minutes each.

Now, to determine the length of the night hours, we will do practically the same calculation. Knowing a day lasts 24 hours, minus the 15 hours of sunlight, we have a total of 9 hours of night or 540 minutes. All we have to do is divide 540 minutes by 12, for the twelve hours of the night, for a total of 45 minutes. In summary, for this example, daytime hours will be 75 minutes long, and nighttime hours will have a duration of 45 minutes. It is as simple as that.

Finally, to perfect my explanation and conclude with this example, if the sun rises at 6:00 am and each planetary day hour has a duration of 75 minutes, we could therefore establish the following:

Daytime Planetary Hours (duration of 75 minutes)	From	To
1st planetary hour	6:00 am	7:15 am
2nd planetary hour	7:15 am	8:30 am
3rd planetary hour	8:30 am	9:45 am
Etc.		

In the same way, we will calculate from the 13th hour the beginning of the night hours knowing that the sunset will take place at 9:00 pm.

Nighttime Planetary Hours (duration of 45 minutes)	From	To
13th planetary hour	9:00 pm	9:45 pm
14th planetary hour	9:45 pm	10:30 pm
15th planetary hour	10:30 pm	11:15 pm
Etc.		

In terms of how to find out when the sun will rise and set, just check a local newspaper. All this information is usually found on the weather page.

While you possess these notions, you must now know when the planet of your choice will be in force during the day or night. Know above all that the first, eighth, fifteenth and twenty-second hour will always be governed by the planet that rules the day. When you will have to practice a ritual or any occult experimentation at the planetary time of a particular star, you will only have to do the calculation that I explained to you, then consult the following chart and choose the planetary time of day or night that will suit you best.

Planetary Hours	☉ Sunday	☽ Monday	♂ Tuesday	☿ Wednesday	♃ Thursday	♀ Friday	♄ Saturday
Day Hours							
1	Sun	Moon	Mars	Mercury	Jupiter	Venus	Saturn
2	Venus	Saturn	Sun	Moon	Mars	Mercury	Jupiter
3	Mercury	Jupiter	Venus	Saturn	Sun	Moon	Mars
4	Moon	Mars	Mercury	Jupiter	Venus	Saturn	Sun
5	Saturn	Sun	Moon	Mars	Mercury	Jupiter	Venus
6	Jupiter	Venus	Saturn	Sun	Moon	Mars	Mercury
7	Mars	Mercury	Jupiter	Venus	Saturn	Sun	Moon
8	Sun	Moon	Mars	Mercury	Jupiter	Venus	Saturn
9	Venus	Saturn	Sun	Moon	Mars	Mercury	Jupiter
10	Mercury	Jupiter	Venus	Saturn	Sun	Moon	Mars
11	Moon	Mars	Mercury	Jupiter	Venus	Saturn	Sun
12	Saturn	Sun	Moon	Mars	Mercury	Jupiter	Venus
Night Hours							
13	Jupiter	Venus	Saturn	Sun	Moon	Mars	Mercury
14	Mars	Mercury	Jupiter	Venus	Saturn	Sun	Moon
15	Sun	Moon	Mars	Mercury	Jupiter	Venus	Saturn
16	Venus	Saturn	Sun	Moon	Mars	Mercury	Jupiter
17	Mercury	Jupiter	Venus	Saturn	Sun	Moon	Mars
18	Moon	Mars	Mercury	Jupiter	Venus	Saturn	Sun
19	Saturn	Sun	Moon	Mars	Mercury	Jupiter	Venus
20	Jupiter	Venus	Saturn	Sun	Moon	Mars	Mercury
21	Mars	Mercury	Jupiter	Venus	Saturn	Sun	Moon
22	Sun	Moon	Mars	Mercury	Jupiter	Venus	Saturn
23	Venus	Saturn	Sun	Moon	Mars	Mercury	Jupiter
24	Mercury	Jupiter	Venus	Saturn	Sun	Moon	Mars

THE SABBATHS: WITCHES' FESTIVALS

THE Sun and the Moon constitute what could be described as being the cosmic hands of a large Earth clock. The ancients have always observed these stars and harmonized with their movements and cycles.

The Sabbaths are all solar in nature; they represent the passage of the seasons marked by the Sun's course on Earth. These annual milestones, honored and celebrated by all witches, are an integral part of the pagan way of life and spirituality. As these come and go perpetually, tradition calls all these cyclical periods the *Wheel of the Year*.

There is a total of eight Sabbaths celebrated by Wicca practitioners. These festivals are divided into two groups; we find the four Greater Sabbaths or Grand Sabbaths, namely the fire festivals Samhain, Imbolg, Beltane and Lughnasadh, as well as four other Celtic solar festivals commonly known as the Lesser Sabbaths, which correspond to the solstices and equinoxes. These eight occasions privileged among the practitioners of the White Art, you can name them Sabbaths, celebrations or festivals, which comes down to the same, reflect on two very distinct and inseparable subjects: the solar theme and that of the fertility of nature.

These concepts symbolize different aspects of the Sun-God and the Moon-Goddess. The Goddess, always present in all the Sabbaths, simply changes her appearance from Mother Earth and her fertility cycles to the Celestial Queen and her lunar cycles. As for the God, for his part, he is characterized by death and resurrection; he dies and is reborn again.

The first theme corresponds to the Sun-God dominating the Lesser Sabbaths. He dies and is reborn on Yule at the time of the Winter Solstice; he becomes mature and impregnates Mother Earth in Ostara during the Spring Equinox; he shines with all his brightness and attains the peak of his glory at Litha, at the Summer Solstice; resigns himself to the power and decreasing influences of Mother Earth at Mabon, during the Autumn Equinox and finally, the cycle ends with the tide of Yule where he dies and is reborn again.

The second theme of nature's fertility is slightly more complex because it involves two figures of God; the God of the Ascending Year, the *Oak King*, as well as the God of the Decreasing Year, the *Holly King*. These are constantly in opposition because they represent light and darkness respectively. These are the twins in perpetual rivalry who conquer and succeed, in turn their reign. They are in eternal competition to obtain the favors of the Great Mother and each in turn, when they reach their peak, they sacrificially mate with the Goddess and die in her embrace to eventually resurrect again when the time comes. Here, light and darkness are explained in terms of complementarity and not in the sense of good and evil. These are the natural phases of the cycle of the year from which life is constantly in perpetual regeneration.

That being said, we will now study each of the Sabbaths in detail as well as their meaning and some of their correspondences which could prove very useful in the context of your personal celebrations.

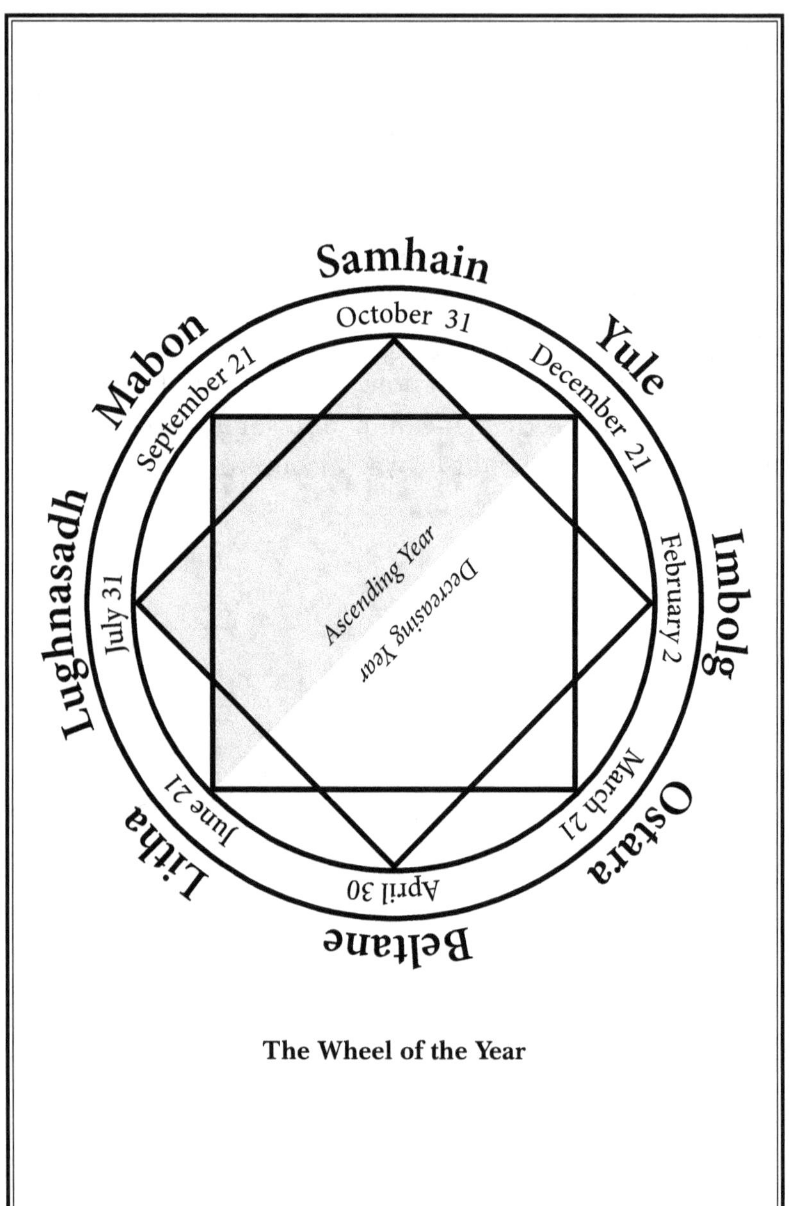

The Wheel of the Year

✵ **Samhain** ✵

October 31ˢᵗ

Samhain (pronounced *'Sow-ein'*) also named by Hallowe'en, All Saints' Day or All Hallows' Day, moment of the third harvest, marks the beginning of the new magickal year and also represents the celebration of the dead. It is the beginning of winter among the Celts and one of the most important festivals (the second being that of Beltane marking the beginning of summer). It is, in addition, the time in the year when the veil between the world from the living and the Other World is the thinnest; humans and spirits can freely cross to the other side without any password because during this night, the door that separates these planes of existence is wide open. In this sense,

Samhain is recognized as a time for divination, for remembering our dearest departed and for communicating with the Spirits of the deceased. Ancestors become more accessible during this period. We also take this opportunity to introspect and reflect on the year that has just ended.

The Wheel of the Year now completes its cycle of life on this privileged day for spirit communion. Samhain is a celebration of the eternal cycle of incarnations and at the same time symbolizes a period of festivities where food and drink are honored as a sign of fertility and life, in defiance at the period of darkness that will occur on Yule. It is also customary to prepare a dish for disembodied souls and the deceased so they can feed themselves on their journey to the Other World.

Sabbath Correspondences

Symbolism: Magickal New Year, the third and last harvest, divination, spirit communication, rebirth beyond death, reincarnation, end of summer, introspection.

Symbols: Pumpkin lanterns, squash, apples, darkness, death, fire, mask.

Goddesses: Hel, Hecate, Ishtar, Inanna, Kali, Keli-De, Macha, Kalma, Lilith, Morrigan, Pamona, Rhiannon, Persephone, Sekhet.

Gods: Arawn, Cernunnos, Hades, Loki, Nefertum,

Osiris, Pluto, Saman, Woden/Odin, Am-Heh, Ghede, Heimdall, Rangi, Xocatl.

Colors: Black, orange.

Incense/oils: Frankincense, myrrh, mint, nutmeg, apple, sage, basil, yarrow, lilac, ylang-ylang, camphor, clove.

Herbs: Pumpkin, chrysanthemum, mugwort, apple, nuts, oak leaves, sage, catnip.

Stones: Jet, obsidian, onyx, carnelian and all black stones.

Sabbatical teas: (individual or blended): Apple cider, angelica, catnip, sage, valerian.

Traditional foods: Apples, turnips, beets, nuts, pumpkin pies, cranberry muffins, mulled wine and cider, poultry, pork.

Altar decoration: Black tablecloth, lanterns carved in pumpkins, photographs of deceased people, apples, autumnal leaves and flowers, nuts, divination tools such as the magick mirror, etc.

✦ **Yule – Winter Solstice** ✦
December 21ˢᵗ

Yule means 'wheel'. The Winter Solstice marks the death and rebirth of the Sun-God; it indicates the victory of the God of the Ascending Year, the Oak King, over the God of the Decreasing Year, the Holly King. The Goddess, personalized at that time as the Queen of the Cold Darkness, now gives birth to the God who will fertilize her again and bring light and warmth once more. On Yule, the two themes of the God coincide perfectly.

Yule is the time of the year when the night is the longest, and from that moment on, the days will begin to lengthen;

the sunshine time will increase day by day. The Solar cycle initiates a new beginning; its power is no longer in decline, but rather continues its race towards its zenith that will take place at the Summer Solstice. Symbolically, the growing child God, the Sun, becomes more and more present by following this same path. It is therefore customary to light large fires, to burn candles or a Yule log (symbolizing the reincarnation of the God by the Goddess) until dawn in order to warmly welcome and celebrate the long-anticipated return of sunlight on Mother Earth.

Sabbath Correspondences

Symbolism: Rebirth of the Sun-God, beginning of the Ascending Year, the longest night of the year, Winter Solstice, establishing plans for the future, the impending return of life and fertility.

Symbols: Yule log, fire, light, holly, fir tree, mistletoe, poinsettia, wheel.

Goddesses: Angerona, Fortuna, Gaia, Heket, Isis, Lucina, Albina, Brigid, Freya, Hannah, Kefa, Ma'at, Nox, Pandora, Thea, Metzli, Tiamat.

Gods: Apollo, Balder, Helios, Janus, Lugh, Mitra, Oak/ Holly King, Ra, Sol, Aker, Attis, Bragi, Hyperion, Mithra, Odin, Marduk.

Colors: Red, green, white, silver and gold.

Incense/oils: Frankincense, myrrh, pine, cedar, cinnamon, nutmeg, rosemary, saffron, ginger.

Herbs: Heliotrope, holly, oak, ivy, mistletoe, laurel, juniper, rosemary, pine, poinsettia.

Stones: Ruby, garnet, emerald, diamond.

Sabbatical teas: (individual or blended): Cinnamon, mullein, willow, yarrow.

Traditional foods: Cumin cookies and cakes, fruit cakes, dried fruits, nuts, turkey, pork, spicy cider, wine, ginger or hibiscus teas.

Altar decoration: Green tablecloth, Yule log, pine or fir branches, pine cones, holly leaves, apples, laurel, juniper, several candles to symbolize the return of light, etc.

✬ **Imbolg** ✬
February 2nd

Imbolg (pronounced *'Im-mol'*), also referred to as Imbolc, Oimelc or Candlemas means 'in the belly'. This Sabbath, this festival of light, rides approximately six weeks after Yule and six weeks before the Spring Equinox. This time of the year is perceived as the fetal state of spring in the bowels of Mother Earth because once again, life is gradually beginning to germinate. This Sabbath also marks the Goddess's recovery after she gave birth to the God at Yule. Imbolg is a derivative of the Gaelic word Oimelc which means 'sheep's milk'. It symbolizes the time when herds of animals give birth to their first offspring or when the milk of life begins to flow into them. Being a festival of fire, like

all the other Greater Sabbaths, Imbolg, however, empha-
sizes the spark of light rather than heat; the light of the
Sun-God that begins to pierce through the dark mantle of
winter preparing to make way for the bright tide of summer.

This Sabbath is associated with Brigid (or Brid), the
Celtic goddess of fire, whose triple nature is also expressed
as a bearer of fertility. It was customary to make straw
crosses in honor of this Goddess as a symbol of protection and prosperity in the forthcoming year. Imbolg is the
propitious time to banish the winter current and embrace
the change of what is obsolete for renewal, from sterility to
conception; we chase what is old making room for novelty.
Imbolg is therefore considered a Sabbath of purifications,
for with the help of the sun's regenerative powers, the time
has come to clean up the energies. Traditionally, it is a very
appropriate period to proceed with initiatory rites and
consequently, personally embark on a new path.

Sabbath Correspondences

Symbolism: Purification, growth and renewal, the rejection of what is old making way for novelty, fertility, first
signs of return to life, personal commitments, initiations.

Symbols: Broom, white flowers, straw cross, candle.

Goddesses: Aradia, Brigid/Brid, Anu, Arachne,
Arianhrod, Athena, Audhumla, Branwen, Dahud, Inanna,

Laufey, Selene, Vesta, Arani, Cardea, Februa, Gaia, Kebechet, Lucina, Triduana, Pax.

Gods: Bannik, Diancecht, Essus, Bragi, Dumuzid, Trusto.

Colors: White, yellow, pink.

Incense/oils: Frankincense, myrrh, basil, laurel, cinnamon, violet, vanilla, olive, carnation, jasmine, rosemary.

Herbs: Angelica, rosemary, willow, clover, laurel, celandine, coltsfoot, heather, iris, violet, and all white and yellow flowers.

Stones: Amethyst, garnet, onyx, ruby, turquoise.

Sabbatical teas: (individual or blended): Chamomile, red clover, rosemary, blackberry.

Traditional foods: Pumpkin and sunflower seeds, poppy seed cake, bread, honey, all dairy products, spicy foods, curry, garlic, leeks, spiced wine and herbal tea, poultry, pork, lamb.

Altar decoration: White tablecloth, white flowers, snow, seeds and grains in an earthy bowl, several white and green candles.

☆ **Ostara — Spring Equinox** ☆
March 21st

The Sun is getting stronger at the coming of the Spring Equinox; the now mature God permeates and fertilizes Mother Earth. Although light and darkness are now in perfect balance on this day of the year, with day and night having precisely the same duration, the light still has the upper hand over darkness and the time of sunshine continues to extend. The Sun-God is gaining more and more power.

Ostara is obviously a Solar festival that symbolizes the rebirth and the return of life. The egg is a symbol associated with this Sabbath; it is the Egg of the World deposited by the Goddess that will hatch under the warm rays of the Sun-God. With the renewal of life, it is time to plant the seeds of our spiritual gardens so that the Earth can fertilize them and maintain their growth until harvest day.

Sabbath Correspondences

Symbolism: Return of spring, fertility of Mother Earth, return to life, balance, the God becomes a man, power of light, time of planting.

Symbols: Eggs, spring flowers, buds, fire, greenery.

Goddesses: Eostre, Ostara, Aphrodite, Athena, Cybele, Eriu, Gaia, Juno, Lady of the Lake, Melusine, Ova, Renpet, Salamaona, Vesta, Astarte, Coatlicue, Flidais, Garbhog, Ishtar, Isis, Minerva, Persephone, Rheda, Venus.

Gods: Cernunnos, the Green Man, Attis, Dagda, Dylan, Mithra, Odin, Ovis, Osiris, Pan.

Colors: Pink, yellow, green, blue, pastel colors.

Incense/oils: Frankincense, myrrh, jasmine, rose, strawberry, lotus, magnolia and all types of flowers.

Herbs: Daffodil, crocus, marjoram, violet, olive, iris, narcissus, woodruff, gorse, peony and all spring flowers.

Stones: Jasper, aquamarine, rose quartz, moonstone.

Sabbatical teas: (individual or blended): Dandelion, hyssop, linden.

Traditional foods: Leafy greens, sprouts, alfalfa, sunflower and sesame seeds, dairy products, nuts, salads, eggs, honey, eggnog.

Altar decoration: Green or white colored tablecloth, flowers on the altar and/or around the magick circle, the cauldron can be filled with water and serve as a flower vase, plants and buds, several candles, everything that represents life and fertility, eggs.

✫ **Beltane** ✫
April 30th

Beltane or Beltaine originally means 'Bright Fire' the fire of the Celtic God known as Bel (Bel meaning 'the bright one'), Beli, Balar or Belenus. The 'bright fires' are lit at the top of the hills to celebrate the return of life and fertility to Earth. In the Celtic tradition, Beltane (as well as Samhain) is one of the two biggest festivals and marks the beginning of summer.

The eve of May is a time of passions, of love hunts; the God and the Goddess are courting each other. The time has come for fertility to bloom after a long winter. Minds are filled with warmth and desires; life pulsates and appetites are awakened. During Beltane, the God finally becomes a man. Exalted by the energies of nature, he desires the Goddess and both fall in love; they unite.

From this union, the Goddess will become pregnant and this omnipresent fertility is once again expressed and celebrated, as it brings new life to the Earth. The vegetation symbolizes the Goddess, while the God is represented by the May tree. Beltane therefore signifies the sacred union, the long-awaited passionate return of vitality and love. As a symbol of the union of the God and the Goddess, ribbons were woven around a maypole (the May tree), the latter representing the Sun-God, while the ribbons symbolized the loving embrace of the Goddess.

Sabbath Correspondences

Symbolism: Fertility, love, renewal of vows, personal growth, union of the Goddess and the God, motherhood of the Goddess, sacred marriages, new lives.

Symbols: Fire, flowers, chalice or cup, love, union, all phallic symbols.

Goddesses: Aphrodite/Venus, Artemis/Diane, Cupra, Blodeuwedd, Damara, Fand, Flora, Hilaria, Mielikki, Prithvi, Rhea, Sarbanda, Skadi, Var, Xochiquetzal, Aima, Ariel, Devana, Erzulie, Flidais, Freya, Lofn, Rhiannon, Shiela-na-gig, Tuulikki.

Gods: Bel/Belenus, Cernunnos, Manawydan, Orion, Puck, Telipinu, Baal, Beltene, Chors, Faunus, Herne, Odin, Pan.

Colors: Red, green, white, dark yellow.

Incense/oils: Frankincense, myrrh, lilac, rose, passion flowers, vanilla.

Herbs: Primrose, hawthorn, rose, rosemary, lilac, birch, all white flowers.

Stones: Emerald, sapphire, rose quartz, blood stone.

Sabbatical teas: (single or blended): Saffron, rose, hibiscus, damiana, burdock.

Traditional foods: Oatmeal cookies or cakes, all dairy products such as cream and cheese, fruit milkshakes and even ice cream.

Altar decoration: White tablecloth, flowers on the altar and/or around the magick circle, the cauldron can serve as a vase with flowers, white and red ribbons.

✫ **Litha — Summer Solstice** ✫
June 21ˢᵗ

At the Summer Solstice, the Sun-God reaches its peak; he is strong, warm and at the zenith of its luminosity. This Sabbath marks the longest day of the year, and from that day on, the time of sunlight unfortunately begins to shorten. The Sun, at the height of its glory, is honored and is asked to bring fertility to the Earth as well as to repel the influences of the darkness that begins a new cycle. For this purpose, bonfires composed of fir and oak were traditionally lit as a celebration of the Sun.

When Litha occurs, the Oak King, God of the Ascending Year, falls into the hands of the Holly King, God of the Decreasing Year and cedes his reign to make way for the progression of darkness and the advent of winter. The Goddess, now very fertile, embraces the Sun-God and also presides over the death of the Oak King.

The Summer Solstice is in addition a time of festivities; nature is lush, the fertility of the Goddess, Mother Earth and the God is at its full capacity. Litha is also recognized as a powerful and extremely favorable time for all magickal practices, regardless of their nature. In the past, witches covered their foreheads during this period with ashes from the fires of Beltane to enhance their magickal powers.

Sabbath Correspondences

Symbolism: The God at his zenith, approaching the harvest, end of the Ascending Year and beginning of the Decreasing Year, the pregnant Goddess, return of Holly King.

Symbols: Summer plants, flowers, fire, oak, sun, wheel.

Goddesses: Aestas, Athena, Aphrodite, Astarte, Ishtar, Damona, Dia Greine, Elat, Erce, Freya, Hathor, Tiamat, Isis, Juno, Nyx, Shekinah, Wurusema, Aine, Artemis, Banba, Dana, Eos, Eriu, Gerd, Grian, Kali, Mebd/Maeve, Mitra, Olwen, Sekhmet, Vesta.

Gods: Baal, Dagda, Dharma, Hadad, Hyperion, Gwydion, Llew, Ra, Thor, Xiuhtecuhtli, Apollo, Balder, Donnus, El, Helios, Legba, Lugh, Oak/Holly King, Prometheus, Sol.

Colors: Red, green, blue, gold.

Incense/oils: Frankincense, myrrh, citrus, rose, cinnamon, lavender, sandalwood, orange, mint.

Herbs: Chamomile, oak, mistletoe, lemon tree, sandalwood, heliotrope, St. John's wort, saffron, laurel, lavender, rose, verbena, honeysuckle, elderberry, thyme, daisy.

Stones: Emerald, jade, lapis lazuli, tiger's eye, diamond.

Sabbatical teas: (individual or blended): Anise, carrot, lemon, orange, nettle.

Traditional foods: Fresh fruits and garden vegetables prepared in various ways, citrus fruits, oranges, lemons, lemonade, beer and mead.

Altar decoration: White tablecloth, summer flowers on the altar and/or around the magick circle, any element of nature that comes from this season.

✶ **Lughnasadh** ✶
July 31ˢᵗ

Lughnasadh (pronounced *'Luhg-na-sah'*), also known as Lammas, means 'the commemoration of Lugh'. Lugh is a god of fire and light, chief of the Tuatha Dé Danann in Irish legends. Among the Anglo-Saxons, the mass in honor of the god Lugh is called Lughomass or Hlaf-mass, which means 'loaf mass', in reference to the harvest of corn and the sacrifice of the Corn King (none other than Holly King).

Lughnasadh is the Sabbath of the first harvest. This is the time to harvest the seeds that the flowers drop for the next sowing. The Sun-God is in decline; he is dying little by little while the Goddess, deeply fertile, now bears the child of her consort. It is a time to celebrate and thank the Earth for its generous kindness and abundance.

Sabbath Correspondences

Symbolism: The first harvest, aging of God.

Symbols: Braided corn and straw doll, horn of plenty, bread, fruits, grains and cereals, fire.

Goddesses: Alphito, Cabria, Ceres, Damia, Freya, Habondia, Ishtar, Persephone, Tailtiu, Taweret, Zara-Mama, Aine, Ashnan, Chicomecóatl, Demeter, Kait, Libera, Nisaba, Taillte, Theia, Zytniamatka.

Gods: Lugh, Bes, Dagon, Liber, Llew, Neper, Xochipilli, Attar, Bran, Lono, Odin.

Colors: Red, gold, yellow, green, orange.

Incense/oils: Frankincense, myrrh, allspice, rosemary, eucalyptus, safflower.

Herbs: Cumin, fern, marjoram, nutmeg, corn, rice, wheat, ginseng, rye.

Stones: Peridot, citrine.

Sabbatical teas: (individual or blended): Alfalfa, goldenseal.

Traditional foods: Loaf of bread, cereals, berries, blackberries, fruits, sheaves of wheat, corn, barley, oats, potatoes, cranberries, all food from the first harvest, cider.

Altar decoration: Yellow tablecloth, sheaves of wheat, barley and oats, fruits and bread, all that represents the first harvest, corn cob doll.

✮ **Mabon — Autumn Equinox** ✮
September 21st

Mabon is a time of balance; day and night are once again equal. Darkness takes over the light; the period of sunlight becomes shorter and shorter. The sleepy Goddess can now rest after having been fertile throughout the year, for here is the time of the second harvest, the grains and the fruits have been gathered. The Sun, though less and less strong, is still present, but the latter is preparing to withdraw in order to regenerate and be reborn from the Goddess again. Nature slowly and quietly withdraws to make way for the quiet calm of the winter season.

The Autumn Equinox represents the completion of the harvests started at Lughnasadh and the gratitude for the abundance obtained and which will be to come. At that time, the warm embrace of the declining Sun-God is worthily greeted, knowing he will soon die, and it is recognized that the Sun and the harvests, men and women, share the same perpetual cycle of rebirth and reincarnation.

Sabbath Correspondences

Symbolism: Second harvest, balance, the spirit world, darkness over light, celebration of wine.

Symbols: Wine, squash, pine cones, acorns, oak leaves, cereals, apples, vines, cornucopia, corn, sun cross.

Goddesses: Cessair, Persephone, Morgana, Nikkal, Ninkasi, Renenutet, Ardvi-Sura, Epona, Lilith, Modron, Ningal, Pomona.

Gods: Dionysus/Bacchus, Haurun, Horned God, Iacchus, Orcus, Hermes, Mabon, Thoth, Thor.

Colors: Brown, orange, purple, red, dark yellow.

Incense/oils: Frankincense, myrrh, benzoin, patchouli, apple blossoms, sage.

Herbs: Acorn, hazelnut, cedar, ivy, vines, hops, tobacco, marigold.

Stones: Yellow topaz, sapphire, lapis lazuli, amethyst.

Sabbatical teas: (individual or blended): All kinds of berries, grapes, heather, hops, sassafras.

Traditional foods: Second crop products, cornbread, cereals, squash, vegetables such as potatoes, beans and onions, beer, wine and apple cider.

Altar decoration: Brown tablecloth, acorns, oak branches, autumn leaves, squash, pine cones, seasonal fruits, corn cobs, etc.

FIFTH PART

Magickal Consciousness

FAMILIARS

Do you remember those old stories of witches and tales to frighten children? You may have noticed that it was often mentioned that they possessed a favorite creature that helped them in their magickal works. These Beings, sometimes cats, sometimes crows or even demonic Entities were magickal characters known as *familiars*.

The familiars were recognized as faithful assistants ready to carry out the witch's orders, obeying each and every word. Although the stories of yesteryear have inevitably tended to slightly alter reality, it nevertheless remains true today that a witch who has formerly worked and sharpened her psychic senses will indeed be able can to give life and possess one, or even several familiars in order to get an impressive helping hand in practical magick. It will be possible, thanks to their help, to remotely perform sometimes even incredible magickal actions. However, in this book, we will not be dealing with negative Entities or demons, be careful! The familiars with whom you will now become acquainted will be of a much more benevolent nature and easier to control than the Elementals or the Spirits of the lower astral.

We will initially see together, the familiars of the animal kingdom, everyone's favorite, then the *synthetic* familiars residing on the subtle planes which that will be alive and created by yourself. In this second case, if you carefully follow my instructions, everything will go smoothly without any pitfalls and you will be able to aspire to obtain very particular and surprising occult results.

☆ The Familiars of the Animal Kingdom

Do you own a pet? If so, you may have a future familiar without even realizing it. If you have a cat, for example, you will likely notice one day that the cat will seem to become curious when you get ready to perform a ritual, as if he wants to participate in it too. It is normal to see this interest in them. Know that animals do not have as many restraints on the psychic level as humans and are therefore much more sensitive to the energies and manifestations of the invisible world. When you set in motion currents of energies and vibrations during practices of witchcraft, they suddenly become alert, perceiving what is happening at a higher level of consciousness.

For my part, among my pets, I have an admirable cat, *Zeta*, and he has an exemplary behavior as a familiar. When I write a book, as throughout the writing of this book of

Magick, he will stand by my side, like at this exact moment, and silently keeps me company. It is like he grasps what I am doing. Moreover, when I transcribe some passages in my grimoire, once again, he stays very close to me, if not literally in my way as he lies directly on the freshly written ink! When I practice exercises of magick development or lie down to attempt an astral projection, he frequently comes and sits immediately next to me and sometimes even straight on my belly, as the faithful guardian of his magician and master. If I practice a ritual, he may come to a corner of my sanctuary to observe me act, carefully following with his big green eyes wide open each of my movements, on the lookout for an ethereal or astral manifestation. Finally, he also perceives the presence of etheric Entities or Beings, like that of my old dragon friend *Pnfyr*.

This reflects in a fair and general way the behavior of a familiar. Of course, there are other demeanors that you will be able to discover eventually, such as the protection an animal can give you and more.

In my humble opinion, we cannot really give a pet a familiar status. He becomes it by himself and chooses too of his own free will. To cite you an example, know that I presently have three cats. And it was only *Zeta*, the one I just mentioned, who seized the opportunity to evolve as my magick companion, the others not seeming to be interested in this type of cooperation. Naturally, I love them all and they reciprocate it back to me very well, but it seems that only one of them has decided to participate and pay special attention to my magickal work. The other cats are more of an independent nature and do not seem to care if I perform a ritual or sit still meditating by candlelight.

Hence, you may have a pet at home, and he may also choose to become your familiar or refuse the opportunity that arises. Under no circumstances can you compel him to act against his will. He is, so to speak, predestined to this magickal cooperation or he is not. Just like you, you are drawn and interested in Magick. Perhaps you have friends or co-workers who do not believe in the occult and pay little attention to it. The same is true for animals. Some will see an opportunity not to be missed, while others will simply do nothing about it.

That being said, you can always try to involve your pet slowly, step by step, in your rites and magickal works. Like a student, try to initiate him gradually. Take him on your lap as you train your witch powers, during a meditation or when you exercise visualization. Gradually get him to practice with you. Be smart, because at first you might have to put a little effort. For example, if your animal has a bed or a basket to lie in, then place the basket in your sanctuary so that he can use it during your next ritual. In this way, he will surely come to be intrigued by your actions and will possibly develop this desire to share other identical moments.

Be resourceful and involve your animal companion more and more in everything you do that will have a magickal or occult connotation. After a few weeks of training, you will see if you have a potential familiar. If you do not obtain any results, you will have to get used to the idea that for the moment, your pet cannot or does not want to become your familiar. Still love him with all your heart and always enjoy his company... he may one day change his mind.

Familiars of the animal kingdom can bring you a lot. If only to keep you company during any ritual, you will appreciate their presence. They detect and capture subtle energies; they stare at a corner of the room as if to signal you that something or someone is there; they share the occult currents and tides; they protect you and warn you of imminent dangers; they accompany you in your work and practices of magickal development and support you in their own way to encourage you to persevere, etc. These are only a few examples among many other advantages that will one day, I hope, be part of your daily life.

Thus, it is true that having the leisure to own a familiar is something truly magnificent, because the collaboration and emotional sharing will be oh how magickal! If you have that opportunity, as I do, then you already know that feeling and that precious bond that I am trying to share with you. If not, do not worry. You will always have the option to practice the ritual contained in this chapter in order to create your own familiar according to your own requirements and needs. Even better, you may as well own both types of familiars; one from the animal kingdom and one (or more) from the invisible world.

☆ How to create your own Familiars

In the unfortunate event of not having the chance to live with a familiar of the animal kingdom or, if you prefer to perform very particular magickal actions, know you can always magickally create your own familiars. They will not be physical like a cat or a bird, but they will be completely autonomous and even more powerful than animals because of their ability to act directly and from the invisible plane.

This technique consists in creating and giving life to an astral Entity through the force of will and visualization by following the ritual prescribed in this chapter. If you have read my book *La Science des Mages*, you will notice that I have already explained a very precise method for creating a similar type of Artificial Entity. However, what follows, even if in some respects the properties will be identical, you will find the ritual technique for obtaining this kind of personal servant is somewhat different and easier to perform while still remaining as satisfying.

Therefore, an Entity with a certain degree of intelligence and autonomy can be consciously created. This Being will live and act on the astral plane and be limited to the execution of the task assigned to him. In other words, you can create one, several, even an army of familiars that will be at your sole service.

Furthermore, when you have given life to your familiar, know that because he will be autonomous and capable to act according to your instructions, any karmic fault committed by such a personal servant will be automatically debited to the hand that manipulates him, namely yourself. This is why one must be cautious when working with astral familiars. For it is true that these creatures will act according to desires and in the name of the witch who controls them. On the other hand, if they make a mistake, it is as if you were the faulty one. Therefore, be extremely careful and remain vigilant.

The more energy you give your familiar, the stronger he will become and the more effective and direct his magickal actions will be. Nevertheless, there may be some gaps with these invisible Beings; indeed, the more strength they receive from the practitioner who created them, the more effective their actions will be, but the more likely they will risk also becoming uncontrollable, due to the fact that they will grow much more powerful and autonomous.

There are many possibilities for the witch as to the use of familiars created by a magickal act. As these will be created according to the wishes and needs of the practitioner, they will be able to accomplish virtually any task. It is enough to just have a need to satisfy and the familiar will have the possibility to make every effort to concretize it on the mental, astral or physical plane. Obviously, this implies it has been formed beforehand according to the Universal Laws that govern magickal actions.

This way you will be able to create a familiar to accomplish various tasks. To give you a starting idea, I will give you a few:

- Increase or decrease at will the intellectual faculties and learning capacity of the practitioner or a third party.
- Increase or decrease courage and strength.
- Increase or decrease vitality and health.
- Change feelings into their opposites; hatred into friendship and friendship into hatred, etc.
- Obtain protection from negative, foreign and hostile influences.

- Subject unto one's will the mind of any individual or animal of his choice.
- Receive and transmit telepathic messages.
- Influence a person's thoughts at will.
- Etc.

Now, before embarking on the practice of this unusual ritual, take the time to properly study the following four rules. The success and the favorable outcome of this magickal experiment depends on it.

The Form attributed to the Familiar

Depending on the assigned purpose, a similar form will be given to the familiar with the help of visualization. There is really no rule to be observed as to the aspect chosen except that the form, or the astral body of the familiar, should have a direct link with the goal and tasks it will have to accomplish. For example, the latter could have the shape of a large ferocious dog or an impressive dragon if it was created to provide protection, defend and stand guard over the witch. In the same vein, if your familiar's mission is to observe what is happening in your surroundings, it could then have the shape of an eagle, a crow or some other bird ready to fly over the desired areas from a distance. Finally, the one who would like to have as familiar an Entity that will influence others in his favor, it could possess the form of an eloquent mage, a devious snake or a cunning and bold fox.

Whatever your personal motives, take the time to reflect on the mission that your future servant will have to fulfill, find the ideal character to carry out this action and give it the corresponding physical form. Remember that your familiar can be human, animal or even alien in appearance if so you desire. It can be as big as a giant or as small as a mouse. Your familiar, your choice.

The Name of the Familiar

To exist, your familiar must imperatively have a name. Without it, the form cannot exist. The name chosen should never correspond with the name of a living or deceased person so that no connection can be made with that individual. It is for this reason that a name invented only for the familiar is more than advised. You will subsequently use this name to summon your servant so that he may manifest himself to you and obey your will.

The Task to accomplish

This is an extremely crucial point not to be taken lightly. What do you want your familiar to accomplish? What does it need to do on your behalf? The task, being the force needed for its realization, will be assigned by the power of will with intense visualization. This task must be clear, obvious, very specific, positive and formulated in the present tense aloud. For example, if you are creating a familiar for protection, do not instill the task in him by saying something like: *'Protect me if I am in danger.'*

You should rather, give the task as a specific function:
'You, (name), protect me against all physical and psychic dangers, at all times of night and day, now, and for as long as you are at my service.'

Time and lifespan

The lifespan of your familiar should also be taken into consideration. For example, you can order your astral servant to dissolve once his task is accomplished. In the absence of pre-established or manual dissolution, your familiar would continue to live and act uncontrollably, even after your death, which would always be karmically bound to you, regardless of his actions. The lifespan is, therefore, one of the most critical points to consider.

☆ The Technical Sheet of the Familiar

Here is, for additional information, the image and technical sheet of a very reliable familiar that I created in the past. It had a humanoid shape without, however having precise features, as if it were only composed of light. SPORASS, of his name, had the function of being imposing, severe and very convincing.

It is recommended to follow the example below and to design a similar sheet in your Grimoire for all your familiars so you can keep track of each of your personal servants.

Familiar's Technical Sheet

Familiar name: SPORASS
Date: March 31, 1999, 10:20 PM
Lunar phase: Full moon
Duration of initial creation: 20 mins.
Time and lifespan: One single occult action.

Appearance: Large muscular being of intense yellowish white light. Arms crossed. Attitude of strength and authority. It has two long horns curved inward on its head.

Purpose and task to be accomplished: ___________

Calling gesture: Hands raised, thumbs between the index and middle fingers say 3 times the name: *'Sporass! Sporass! Sporass!'*

Sending gesture: Give the order in a dry tone and aloud to go and act on the mind of the person by pushing with the hands outwards, then clapping them immediately, all done very quickly and forcefully.

Successful occult action: Yes, with success.

Familiar SPORASS, as illustrated by the author

✯ **Ritual of the Familiar** ✯

- Sit comfortably and meditate for a short time in order to completely clear your mind of any wandering thought. When you feel ready to begin the ritual technique of familiar creation, continue.

- Visualize that you are standing in front of a huge ocean of light. See this light penetrate you; it is brilliant in all its brightness and infinite.

- When you will be able to clearly see in your mind this ocean of light, start compressing it into the chosen shape of your future familiar. Gradually compact this light and give it the physical appearance of your creature. The more the light is condensed, the more it will increase in intensity, like the power of ten thousand suns. Slowly your familiar takes shape.

- Finally, after an intense visualization, you should see your formed familiar standing in front of you, in the right size and dimensions. At this stage of your occult work, the familiar must be perfectly shaped, standing still and silent. Take your time to contemplate it in all its details.

- Now, charge and transfer your powerful will to your familiar; that is, imbue him strongly and mentally with the task which it will soon have to accomplish for you.

This step is extremely important. Take all your time to perfectly inculcate your will into the creature standing in front of you.

- When the familiar has received his instructions by the force of your mind about what it was created to do, you will give him his name by saying aloud: *'You are (name)! You are (name)! You are (name)!'*

- Now is the time to determine the lifespan of your familiar. Do you want it to dissolve as soon as its work is done or do you want it to stay alive so that it can be on duty several times if necessary? Recite the task assigned to him, mentioning the duration of the action to be carried out. For example: *'You, (name), change into love the hatred that so-and-so feels towards me and as soon as this task is accomplished, you will return to the ocean of light from which you came.'* If your familiar needs to have a longer life, you can also specify that it will always become stronger day by day, etc.

- The name, task and time duly assigned, know that if you have practiced this ritual consciously, with all the strength of your will and visualization, you have truly given birth to an astral Entity, which is now ready to obey your orders. Tell your familiar that when you pronounce his name, accompanied by this or that calling gesture, it will be obliged to present itself to you to obtain new instructions.

- Launch your familiar so that it can immediately go and execute its task.

- The ritual is now complete. Let your familiar act and no longer think about it so that it can more easily work and serve you. Remember, in the event that the specified lifespan is longer than a single action, you will need to feed your familiar with your vital force in order to increase its power of action. To do this, call it on a regular basis and when it will be standing in front of you, transmit it some of your energy by the strength of your will and your visualization.

DIVINATION TECHNIQUES

ONE of the most interesting aspects of Magick, not to say the most attractive is undoubtedly everything that directly or indirectly relates to divination. For centuries, magicians, occultists and witches have turned to divinatory techniques in order to be able to predict quite accurately what the future might hold. Among these methods, we find the most popular including tarot, I-Ching, crystals and crystal balls, runes, magick mirrors and so on.

The primary reason why I wish to teach you the two techniques of divination contained in this chapter is to give you an additional tool in practical magick. This tool will allow you to see or get a glimpse of what your occult work could bring to you in terms of results in order to detect whether a ritual does indeed have its purpose. Sometimes you will realize that practicing this and that a ritual could greatly enhance your fate... but will it really be so? This is what divination will allow you to discover.

In other words, as I know for a fact that you will give yourself wholeheartedly in the practice of your witchcraft rituals, I think it would be therefore preferable, for your well-being (and that of others), to be able to know if the actions you wish to take will be relevant, whether they can truly express your hopes and if they will prove to be just and thoughtful.

It is of course understood that you will always be able to practice divination in other circumstances and not only to verify the possible results of your rituals. You likely have questions about some aspects of your life. However, if you wish to obtain answers, once again, divination may prove very useful, not only for you, but also for your loved ones or anyone else who needs to inquire about your services.

In addition, we must also be careful not to confuse "divination" and "fortune-telling". Fortune-telling is saying this or that thing *will happen*. Where on the other hand, divination will indicate that a given situation is *likely to occur* provided that you continue on the same path that you are on now.

With this in mind, you always have the free will to wait for it to happen or prevent it; to let the situation manifest itself or to circumvent it by opting for another direction to follow or by taking different actions.

Predicting fortune-telling would mean, for example, that on a given day at a specific date, you will have an unfortunate car accident. While on the divination side, you would rather be told than driving your car at this time could cause you some trouble or even an accident, and that it would be advisable to avoid using it. You would therefore have the choice, following this warning, to abstain from driving or to be extremely careful on the road.

Thus, unlike fortune-telling, which advocates the future in reference to predestination, divination, on the other hand, indicates what might wait at the end of the road in terms of probabilities, leaving you free will to face a possible situation or prevent it by taking action accordingly.

It is my humble opinion that predicting fortune-telling makes no sense for the future is constantly changing. Remember: a needle cannot fall without upsetting the entire Universe... One action will cause repercussions, while another may produce diametrically opposed effects. Consequently, in this book it will be treated only of divination; the art of seeing what the future may hold.

☆ Magick Mirror Divination

The magick mirror acts as a portal or a kind of threshold between the physical world and the astral plane. It is truly a window to the other dimensions. Such a tool can therefore efficiently project what is on the other side of the subtle veil. It will be possible for you with a magick mirror to see, as much in terms of clairvoyance, as to proceed to divination in order to receive information.

I have extensively covered the subject of magick mirrors and how they are made in *La Science des Mages*. If you are interested in learning all the possible techniques, ranging from clairvoyance to astral travels, and the uses that can be made of them in Magick, I cannot do otherwise but recommend that you to read it.

That being said, a magick mirror is typically made of black glass. Instead of telling you here how to make this type of mirror, I will instead encourage you to use one of your magick tools that can be employed for essentially the same functions, that is, the cauldron.

Indeed, if you use your magick cauldron or even just a plain bowl of dark color, you will succeed in obtaining a basic mirror that will prove effective for divinatory purposes. To make a magick mirror using your cauldron, fill it with pure water at full capacity and place it in the center of your altar. Light two candles and place them on each side, being careful that the light is not reflected on the surface of the water. It is as simple as that; you are now ready.

Take place in front of your magick mirror and adopt a comfortable position. Now gaze at the water and try to get that feeling of depth, as if you were able to look on the other side of that dimension, deep into that dark surface. Without unnecessarily straining your optic nerves, that is, by passively contemplating the mirror, think strongly about your question, then, ask it out loud as follows:

What will be the result if I use Magick to achieve...?

Look at the surface of the water, always remaining neutral and stay very attentive. Allow the manifestations come to you without ever forcing them. Usually at first, you will have the impression that the surface of the mirror suddenly covered with a kind of dark cloud of gaseous vapor. Then you will be able to see energy forms, colors and luminous spots twirling and moving in all directions in a fluid and ethereal way.

Gradually, with practice and depending on the degree of development of your psychic senses, the surface of your magick mirror will become clearer and you will start to see bits of images and slightly blurred scenes. These manifestations will often be bizarre and inconsistent, difficult to understand or interpret. The more you practice, the more limpid and precise your visions will become. Sooner or later, you will be able to understand what you have seen.

I do not wish to delve into the subject any further because not everyone will find it easy to perform divination with this method. This requires training and developed psychic abilities. Nevertheless, try your own experiments and if you get very little success, then move on to the next divinatory technique, which is much easier while being just as effective.

☆ Tarot Divination

Tarot divination is an ancient art that possibly goes back to ancient Egypt. There are historical facts dating as far back as the 14th century. Regardless of its origins, because this is not the purpose of this practical work, tarot remains today an effective divinatory technique, easy to use and very popular.

There are on the market, countless quantities of divinatory oracles and of the most diversified tarot decks. When the time comes to get one, you will really be spoilt for choice. Choose it by letting yourself be guided by your own intuition and personal tastes. Look at the cards and be inspired by them. You will certainly find the deck that will be made for you and that will suit you.

A standard tarot deck consists of 78 cards. These cards are divided into two arcana; the Major Arcana, consisting of 22 cards and the Minor Arcana, with 56 cards. In this chapter, I will teach you a divinatory technique using only the Major Arcana. These 22 cards tend to represent forces in perpetual change and offer broad guidelines for future events, while the Minor Arcana rather indicates static forces and provides more precision with complementary information.

It is true that a divinatory reading using all the cards will be more accurate and detailed, but the use of the Major Arcana alone, besides being easier, will provide you with more information about how events change or will change sooner or later in your life.

We will now see how to use tarot for divinatory purposes. To read your draw, you will use the layout of the "open hexagram" as shown in the following figure.

This layout shows two triangles consisting of three cards each with a seventh card in the center. The upper triangle represents the spiritual forces in manifestation on the earthly plane. As for the lower triangle, it indicates conscious and unconscious desires and what you really want or need. Finally, the last card in the center represents the answer to your question, the verdict of your divination, the outcome if you keep walking the same path.

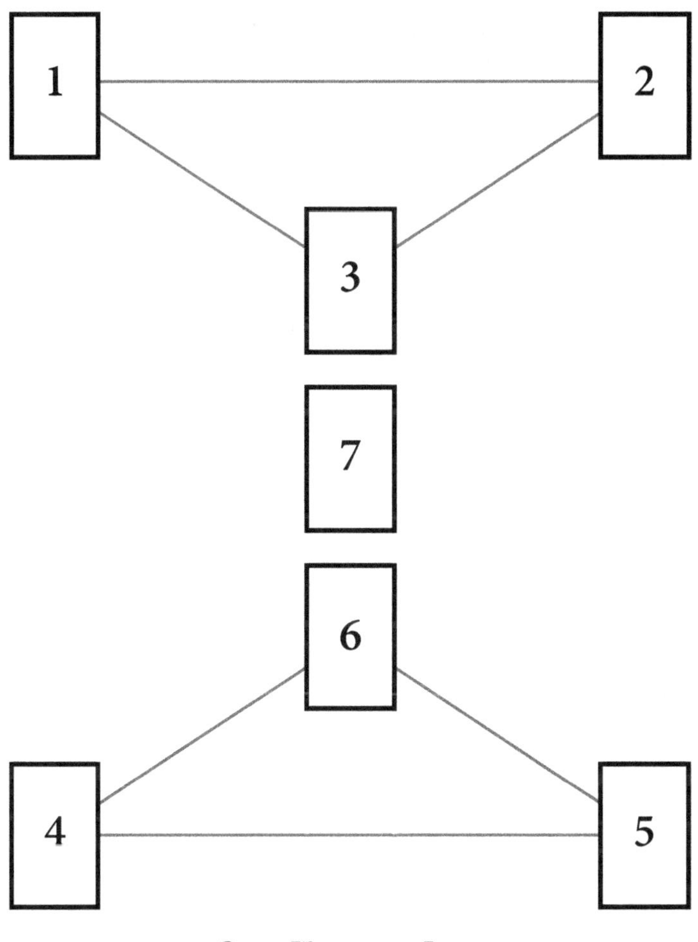

Open Hexagram Layout

To discover the likely results of your magick or for any other area of your choice requiring clarification, whether it is for you alone or to help a third party, use the following technique.

☆ **Divinatory Technique by the Major Arcana** ☆

- With your Tarot Deck in hand, start by removing the Minor Arcana and leave it aside. Bundle up with the 22 Major Arcana cards.

- Place your deck of cards flat in front of you and place your right hand on it. Now put your question out loud clearly and precisely, without ambiguity. For example, in the case of divination to detect the results of a ritual:

What will be the result if I use Magick to achieve...?

- While concentrating mentally and firmly on your question, shuffle the cards in the way you choose, making sure they can be well mixed and that some of them can also be turned upside down. You can, for example, mingle them directly flat on your altar in a circular way, then stir them in your hands.

- Form the deck back together and place it in front of you again. Remember to always focus on the question this whole time. Then cut the cards into three different packs and collect them up from right to left.

- Take the first card from the top and place it in position 1, face down. Continue this way to form the first upper triangle (cards 1, 2, 3). Move on by placing the cards to form the lower triangle (cards 4, 5, 6). Then, finally, place the last card (7) in the center of the two triangles, still according to the hexagram diagram.

- Now turn over cards 1 and 2. These represent the *unknown spiritual influences*. Card 2 will be more related to you than the first card. Its influence is closer to you. Interpret the first two cards.

- Turn the third card (3). This represents the *spiritual advice* in this matter concerning you, about the question for which you are making this divination. Once again, interpret this card.

- Turn card 4. The latter represents your *unconscious desire*. This card will indicate the real hidden motive that drives you to act. What is the unconscious reason behind your conscious reason. Here, you may notice your apparent motives for performing a ritual may not coincide with your unconscious desire. Interpret this card.

- Turn the card 5. It represents your *conscious desire*. What you believe or desire to achieve with your Magick. Interpret this last card.

- Now turn over card 6. This indicates the *practical advice* in full knowledge of the facts. This card can therefore demonstrate or suggest to you to change your perspective in order to attain the goal you have set for yourself and what you really want to achieve. Or, this sixth card can advise you to continue on the same path or to abandon your current project. In any case, this is only an opinion; it is up to you and you alone to follow it and take action according to your conscience. Interpret the card.

- Finally turn the last and seventh card (7). This card shows the answer to your question, the end result if you continue on this same path. Be aware that even if your reading with the previous cards indicated until now a positive avenue, the latter can nevertheless inform you that the result could still be negative. I would like to clarify here that divination with the help of the Major Arcana by the arrangement of the hexagram offers very quick, effective and good results, but that they may not always take into consideration all the subtle implications involved in the matter. This is why sometimes you will be unable to immediately grasp the answers to your questions. Interpret this last card.

- Make a global summary of your divinatory reading to get an overview of the answer you got.

Example of divination

To give you a good idea of a divination with the Major Arcana, here is a concrete example that can help you to know how to properly interpret a drawing of cards.

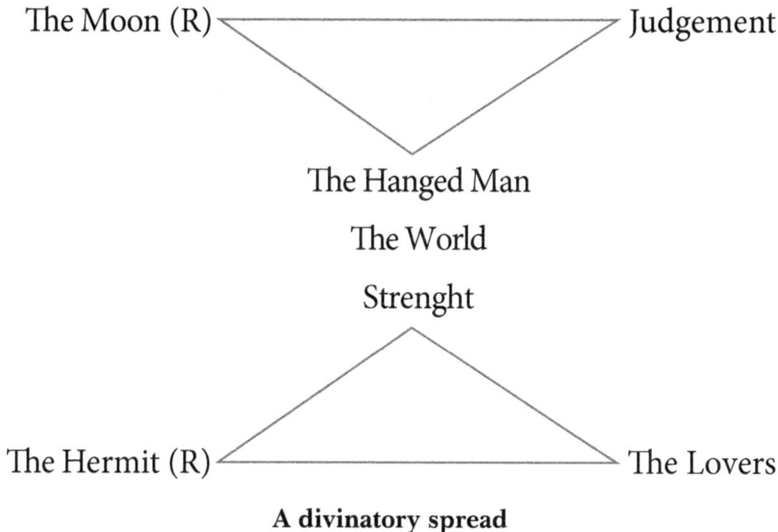

A divinatory spread

Let's imagine for example, that I wish to proceed with
a divination to find out if practicing a ritual to obtain love
in my life will bring the expected fruits. After I shuffle and
draw the cards, I get the following:

- Cards 1 and 2 tell me that this ritual would lead me to
  a period of change and renewal (Judgment) but that I
  am currently blocking myself from this coming because
  of perhaps old disappointments (The Moon reversed).

- Card 3 (The Hanged Man) indicates this ritual could
  lead me to wisdom if I can make sacrifices.

- Card 4 (The Hermit reversed) shows that I am unconsciously too cautious and fearful to get what I want.

- Card 5 (The Lovers) indicates I consciously desire love and affection in my life.
- Card 6 (Strength) gives me a practical advice to have confidence in my abilities and to show inner strength to achieve my goal and that I will need to be kind and attentive.

- The final result indicated by Card 7 (The World) demonstrates that my ritual is meant to be successful and that I will obtain full satisfaction.

Practice by dedicating yourself daily to divination. Also try to remember the meaning of the cards. You can, for example, study one card a day and, over time, you will know their full meaning by heart. Be aware that you will need to be a little patient before you get concrete results and accurate readings. The more you use the tarot, the more you will become experienced and familiar with the cards and their meaning. The more you practice, the more accurate and precise your readings will be. As with any discipline, even in Magick, success is not instantaneous. It comes from working and exercising. Remember; practice makes perfect!

)O(

✫ **Divinatory Meaning of the Major Arcana** ✫

0— THE FOOL: Recklessness, extravagance, impulses and spontaneity, unpredictability, letting go of emotions, wonder. (Reversed) Hesitation, difficulty letting go of instincts, fear of the unknown.

I— THE MAGICIAN: Abilities, will and consciousness, personal confidence, power, control, creativity and energy, concentration, transformation of old situations and advent of novelties. (Reversed) Misuse of personal power, lack of skills, blockage of energies, resistance, arrogance.

II— THE HIGH PRIESTESS: Science, knowledge and awareness, education, time for tranquility and silence, introspection, search for peace, use of intuition. (Reversed) Ignorance, superficial knowledge, a time for action and commitments.

III— THE EMPRESS: Maternal figure, abundance, action, creativity, joyful activities, passion and sensuality, love of nature. (Reversed) Inaction, loss of power, blocking of passions, difficulty of expression.

IV— THE EMPEROR: Power, efficiency, reason, influence of society, rules and laws, insensitivity, sexual power. (Reversed) Immature emotions, obstructions of plans and possibilities, development of sensitivity.

V — THE HIEROPHANT : Mercy and kindness, a person who demonstrates these qualities, traditions and belief systems, teachings, conformity and group. (Reversed) Weakness, social pressures, doctrines and ideas that have lost their meaning, originality.

VI — THE LOVERS : Love, friendship, feelings, relationships, a new love, a test to pass. (Reversed) A failed test, a lost love, end or troubles in a relationship, lack of love, insecurity and loneliness.

VII — CHARIOT : Triumph, overcoming obstacles, will and power in solving problems, endurance, victory over fears. (Reversed) Defeat, insurmountable obstacles, lack of will, passivity and weakness.

VIII — STRENGTH : Spiritual power, inner strength, trust, compassion and kindness. (Reversed) Blockage of power, incapacity and despotism, weaknesses, being distraught.

IX — THE HERMIT : Gain of wisdom, precautions, spiritual advancement, withdrawal from external interests and introspection, personality development, powerful dreams. (Reversed) Fears, excess of caution, lack of wisdom in the actions taken, fear of loneliness, bad dreams, not wanting to grow.

X — WHEEL OF FORTUNE : Good fortune, success, luck, changing circumstances, taking your life in hand, faith.

(Reversed) Difficulty adjusting to change, resistance to change, bad luck, bad fortune.

XI— JUSTICE: Justice, balance and equilibrium, analyses, examining and correcting one's life in balance. (Reversed) Imbalance, acting unfairly, trying to avoid or evade an honest assessment.

XII— THE HANGED MAN: Wisdom resulting from personal sacrifice, attachment, deep spiritual awareness, independence. (Reversed) Selfishness, being influenced by external ideas, pressure to conform and blend in with the crowd, lack of goals.

XIII— DEATH: Evolution through change or transformation, transition, death and end of a cycle. (Reversed) Resistance to change, stagnation, inertia, difficulty letting go.

XIV— TEMPERANCE: Temperance, unions and combinations, taking control, moderation. (Reversed) Acting to the extreme, excessive behavior, being out of control.

XV— THE DEVIL: Something must happen and eventually for good. Something exciting and possibly dangerous or forbidden, temptations, explorations of darker feelings. (Reversed) Something must happen and possibly for evil, resist temptations, bad times for sensuality, fear of own decisions.

XVI— THE TOWER: Ruin, catastrophe, destruction, fall, crisis, situation that can lead to disaster if it continues, increasing pressure, buried emotions resurfacing. (Reversed) Identical meaning, but to a lesser degree.

XVII— THE STAR: Hopes and optimism, promising future, reality and feeling, humility. (Reversed) Disappointed hopes, pessimism, fear of the future, tension and anxiety, isolation.

XVIII— THE MOON: Deceptions, hidden enemies, duplicity, imagination, fantasies, creativity. (Reversed) Minor disappointments, conscious thinking blocking the unconscious.

XIX— THE SUN: Enlightenment, joy and contentment, wonderful life, excitement, optimism, confidence. (Reversed) Loss of confidence, frustration, identical meaning, but to a lesser degree.

XX—JUDGMENT: Renewal, rebirth, in view of a period of change, seeing things differently. (Reversed) Delay and waste of time, resistant to change.

XXI— THE WORLD: Assured success, fulfilment, plenitude, satisfaction, remission of diseases, the life that opens before us. (Reversed) Failure, inertia, bad reward, stagnation and limitations, resistance or opposition.

RITUALS IN PRACTICAL MAGICK

MAGICK is a way of life; it is a way of seeing the Universe in all its splendor with a keen eye, while showing spiritual openness. Magick is the Science of sciences; it is rightly the study and application of the Cosmic and occult Laws of nature.

But even more, Magick is also an eminently practical means to change the course of things by applying accurately and righteously the precepts of the White Art. I mentioned to you at the beginning of this book that eventually, ritual practice would become an integral part of your life. However, to be able to carry out a magickal operation in practical witchcraft, one must be able to know the functioning of rituals in order to be capable to adequately create and apply them.

So far in this book of witchcraft, you have seen how to develop some of your psychic abilities and senses, in addition to have assimilated (I hope) a good deal of important and vital information about the workings of the Universal Laws that govern our world and White Magick.

That being said, have you ever noticed how many magickal recipe books there are on the market? How easy it had become to obtain simplistic rituals in order to meet an ever-increasing number of needs? Do you sincerely believe you need about thirty different love rituals to obtain love and affection? That if a ritual does not work, then the hell with it, I still have others in store? Do you think it is essential to have books and books explaining how to obtain by magick more money and wealth?

Well no, this is not necessary!

Think carefully about the following statements. If you know the Cosmic and Universal Laws, if you know our world is made of vibrations and that you can, through them, apply a subtle pressure to charge this energy in such a way as to bring it to manifestation on the physical plane of matter, if therefore by respecting and enforcing these laws you know how to express a desire for it to be fulfilled... Do you really think you need thirty different methods to achieve it? Absolutely not.

If you know the secret, you only need one way to get there or, if you prefer, only one ritual.

If this method is practiced correctly, it will only act each time by producing the same expected effects. This explains why this book, intended to be complete, contains very few magickal rituals. The reason is quite simple; you do not need more.

Thus, you will be able to practice the rituals contained

in the last part of this book as often as the need arises. On the other hand, if you have a specific need that you wish to magickally correct with the help of a ritual that I omitted to transmit to you, as you will agree, I simply could not write a ritual for all the problems on Earth, you can then refer to the next chapter since this is its *raison d'être*. You will learn how to build your own rituals based on the rules of the Art. In this way, you will be capable to design all your rituals in practical witchcraft, with the assurance that they will be perfectly operational and effective, following the same steps that I will now explain to you.

☆ Rituals Dynamics

Practicing a magickal ritual is one thing. Knowing how a ritual works is another. It is said of incantations in barbaric language that if you want them to bring the desired results, it is imperative to know in the first place what the words that will be uttered mean. It is the same for rituals. It is necessary to know how to recognize the forces in action and, in addition, comprehend how they will operate when they are awakened by an act of Magick. To avoid burdening this chapter with too technical or complex explanations, I will try to explain the main points in all simplicity.

You will notice that very few books on Magick thoroughly explain the proper functioning of the rituals they present. As if merely putting them into practice was enough to achieve results, as if I said that laying paint on a canvas was enough to produce a work of art. Have you ever wondered whether, if you were performing a particular ceremony, how it could act on the invisible planes? How did the effects of the ritual end up bringing the fruits of your labors? Why such and such candle colors or specific incense, plants and herbs? I am convinced that if this question has not already crossed your mind, it undoubtedly will do so in the near future, when your thirst for knowledge becomes greater. From that moment on, you will begin to *deconstruct* the rituals that you will find in books of Magick in order to discover all their meaning, if any, and the common thread.

Magickal rituals in witchcraft are in a sense, a theatrical way to invigorate an energetic force, a vibration, an occult current or a form of energy-power. They are the means by which you present yourself humbly and pure in body and mind before the God and the Goddess in a sacred place dedicated to the application of your knowledge and Universal wisdom.

Practicing magick therefore means working with terrestrial, subtle, planetary, spiritual and/or Universal energies and currents. Everything is interrelated, remember that. Hence how do we come to work with energies? Generally speaking, we could say that the seed of an idea comes from the mental plane. This idea germinates slowly and quietly in your mind. That is when you say to yourself that performing a ritual for this or that cause would probably be more than desirable.

This thought continues on its way, constantly returning to your head. You think about it and give it more energy at the same time. Thus, the idea becomes progressively significant and remains in survival in your mind. Eventually, this initial idea becomes increasingly more intense. You now feel a much more precise need; practicing a ritual to succeed in modifying something or a very specific situation. You tell yourself that if you do the ritual your life will change and everything is going to be fine. The mental force of departure has begun its descent into the planes of existence. It is now strengthened and presently sits in the astral plane, the plane of emotions.

In the same way, by always receiving your energy through your feelings becoming more and more intense, this force will ultimately begin the last phase of its descent and will materialize on the physical plane of matter and so, you move on to the execution the ritual.

This explains in a quick and lighter way the mechanics of an action taking into account the energies set in motion in the subtle planes. Know that this is unconsciously experienced for any action and not only in Magick.

Now that we know a little better how the energetic descent of a forthcoming manifestation takes place in a person, we will at this time look at the functioning of rituals in Magick and the important points to remember. As you will soon see, the principle is essentially the same in both cases; everything is, and will always remain, a matter of currents of energies and vibrations.

☆ How to Create Rituals: The Eleven Rules to Follow

I would say there are substantially as many ways of performing a ritual as there are witches in this world, each having developed over time his own method of conceiving his rites. However, there will always be a way to operate that will bring the desired success in practical Magick. This is a guideline that will take into consideration the *vibratory aspect and analogies* of the forces of the Universe.

If you scrupulously follow this technique of ritual elaboration, you can be convinced that your magickal actions, whatever they may be, will always be carried out effectively because these will respect the occult Laws of nature and the Cosmos that govern manifestations, whether physical, astral or mental.

There are eleven basic rules to follow to effectively create and design a ritual in practical witchcraft. They are:

1. The purpose of the ritual
2. The powers at stake
3. The Sphere of existence or planet
4. The lunar phase
5. The planetary day
6. The planetary hour
7. The color of magickal lamps
8. The magickal incense and bath formula
9. The verb, the incantations and the invocations
10. Preparation of the magick temple
11. Personal preparation

Let us now turn our attention to each of these rules individually, in order to fully understand their implications in Magick.

1. The purpose of the ritual

The first consideration to take; the force behind the action; the purpose of the ritual. Take the time to examine the matter and think about what you want to achieve. Please, always be reasonable in your requests! If you want to practice a ritual to become wealthy or at ease, do not try becoming rich through Magick. It will never work.

The purpose of the ritual must be something possible and achievable. You will have to think about what you want to obtain in simple, clear, precise terms, and always respecting the free will of others. If, for example, you want to get love in your life, do not think about a specific person falling in love with you. The purpose of the ritual should rather be that the person made for you and who will bring you the love you seek manifests himself in your life.

If you need a financial boost, again, do not ask for the wealth of kings. Instead, ask money barriers to be removed from you and for contracts or a raise in recognition of your good work, for example, ask for monetary abundance and so on.

Write down the purpose of your ritual if necessary and consider whether it makes sense and right for you. Is it a purely egocentric and selfish desire? In essence, weigh the pros and cons. When you have clearly set the goal of the latter, if any, continue with the second rule.

2. The powers at stake

Here is where your research work on vibrations resonating in sympathy with your desire begins. What specific force, if any, your ritual should use? Do you wish to involve the energy-egregore of a deity, a god or a goddess, or a particular Cosmic Element? What kind of strength and energy is your ritual supposed to awaken and manifest?

Find out what Universal force vibrates in perfect analogy with your ritual. What is this power that best expresses the goal you have set for yourself and which you eagerly desire to achieve through ritual practice.

Unfortunately, I could not cite you several examples. You will have to make some efforts on your own to find the type of power you want to charge your lens of power; your magick circle.

3. The Sphere of existence or planet

A ritual should always be aligned with a Sphere of existence or a celestial body. Knowing that by reproducing the vibrations of these, you will be able to charge your magickal temple with a force that will obviously be linked to your desire to fulfill. This Sphere of existence can be Celestial and spiritual, like the Universal light; elemental like Fire, Air, Water and Earth or planetary.

For all these Spheres, as we have seen previously in the case of the planets, the latter contains powerful, well-defined vibratory forces. Each has influences and auspices that you can use to create an energetic channel and a vibratory atmosphere in accordance with a magickal ritual. By doing so, you will greatly increase the power of all your rites.

You must now continue to align specific vibrations that will be in perfect analogy with the purpose of the ritual. Find the energy that expresses what you desire. If you choose a planetary Sphere, refer to the fourth part of this book, the chapter dealing with *Influences and Correspondences of the Planetary Spheres*, and determine which will be most appropriate to generate a flow of energy corresponding to the goal you wish to achieve.

4. The lunar phase

As with rule number 3, you should also keep an eye on the appropriate lunar phase to practice your ritual. Knowing from the outset that the moon also possesses and emits an energy field, determine by consulting the corresponding chapter, which is the ideal lunar phase favoring the obtaining of the best possible results. Some will say that if we only respect the Spheres of existence, this may be enough to carry out a magickal operation. In some cases, that may turn out to be right. Nevertheless, the purpose of this chapter is to teach you how to best develop a magickal ritual. However, always try as much as possible, to comply with the eleven basic rules. The more you respect these precepts of the Art, the better your chances of success will be.

5. The planetary day

Having previously determined the planetary Sphere that vibrationally expresses your desire, you will immediately know what is the ideal time of the week to practice your ritual. Sunday for the Sun, Monday for the Moon, Tuesday for March, etc.

6. The planetary hour

You now know it is possible to multiply the power of your rituals by working at the right moments, that is, when the planets analogous to your desires will be in force during the day or night. Therefore, regarding your future ritual, once you have established the dominant planetary Sphere for the purpose of your occult action, you will need to determine the favorable planetary hours in order to know the best time to take action, making the most of these magickal influences. You will notice that you can work either during the day or at night. This choice is very personal, so it is up to you to decide the most suitable time.

7. The color of magickal lamps

The seventh rule to follow is to determine what color your magickal lamps will be. Remember what was said about light. Light plays an important role in Magick as a vibratory transmitting agent. The light produced by one or more magickal lamps emits an energetic field, a specific subtle frequency which, depending on the color of the light used, generates a particular vibration that will resonate in perfect harmony, even in sympathy, with a given Intelligence or Sphere of existence.

Being aware that the nature of the Celestial Spheres is expressed by the graduation of the luminous brilliance, you will want to use lamps or if needed be, candles of the same color as your desire, referring to the chapter dealing with the magickal and vibratory correspondences of the colors. Normally, you will use the same color as the Sphere of Existence that governs your ritual.

8. The magickal incense and bath formula

You should always use an incense composition to burn during a ritual to properly adjust the vibratory atmosphere of your magickal temple, the sacred place where you will practice your rituals. Even better, using the same mixture together and practicing a magick bath beforehand would be ideal.

For this purpose, you can use a basic incense or a specific mixture, or even both at the same time. Refer to the section of *plant compositions for magick baths and incense* to find the mixture that will be most suitable for your ritual practice.

9. The verb, the incantations and the invocations

While this rule may be considered optional, perhaps you like to use the power of the verb during your ritual. By creating calls or invocations, your consecrated words will constitute the incantation to be pronounced during a specific stage of the ritual. Whether it is a question of invoking and evoking the presence of an Entity or a deity, of declaring your will or even, as a mantra, simply intoxicating your mind in order to raise yourself to a higher level of consciousness to allow you to connect to the required vibrations, you can then be able act in the invisible by having at your fingertips the use of the creative verb.

Meditate conscientiously on the words to be spoken and align yourself appropriately with the frequency and impact that your incantations should have. You will thus have the possibility of building a vortex of energies that will be associated with the very nature of the ritual in question, which will manifest your will in concrete facts.

10. Preparing the magick temple

This step consists in making the final preparations to carry out your occult operation. The preparation of your sanctuary ranges from the layout of your altar and magickal tools, the equipment you will need if you have to craft charms, to the grand energetic cleaning of your workplace.

In other words, always start by cleansing and purifying your magick temple, not only physically but also psychically. For this purpose, you can practice a banishing ritual such as the highly effective LBRP (Lesser Banishing Ritual of the Pentagram). Otherwise, you can still fumigate a purification composition for about fifteen minutes (see the purification and exorcism compositions). Then arrange your sanctuary properly, place your tools on your altar, your candlesticks, your accessories, your ceremonial robe so that you do not forget anything and that everything is ready to begin the magickal ceremony. All that remains is to purify yourself and you will be good to go about the ritual practice.

11. Personal Preparation

Last but not least. The eleventh rule not to be neglected; the purification of the operator. Indeed, it is more than advisable to get rid of the negative psychic influences and vibrations that you have accumulated over the course of the day before practicing a ritual so as not to carry them around with you and spread all kinds of impurities in your sacred temple.

Though, a purifying immersion is therefore essential before starting any type of ritual. If you are limited in time, a quick and conscious shower will do the trick. Respect the God and the Goddess at all times. Present yourself to them pure in body and mind.

You may surely notice that I have frequently used terms that correspond to *vibratory frequencies*. It is easy to understand this intentional repetition when we recognize the crucial importance of this Universal Law of analogy on the manifestation on the earthly plane.

Here is what the rules of the Art consist of in the elaboration of rituals in practical witchcraft. Apply them in your daily life, whenever you want to conceive a ritual. If you follow these steps one by one, it is certain and beyond any doubt that you will achieve the desired success, as long as you practice your rites conscientiously employing the six basic pillars constituting your magickal powers as a witch.

Now that it has been unveiled the ground rules to follow for creating rituals, I will now offer you an outline, a structure or if you prefer, a procedure to follow, so that you can get a general idea on how a magickal operation in practical witchcraft could theoretically take place. Please know that you are not required to comply fully. You will therefore be able to make your own modifications to make this outline a little more personalized. Either way, if you think you need some structure, then the following will definitely give you a good starting point.

☆ **Ritual Outline for Practical Witchcraft** ☆

Opening of the Ritual
- Tracing the magick circle.
- Invocation to the God and the Goddess.
- Calling the Watchtowers and their Elements.

Call of the deities to invoke & manifestation of Spheres of existence or planet
- Manifestation and adjustment of the vibratory atmosphere through the use of magickal lamps and incense fumigations.
- Use of the Verb and Incantations to call and manifest a particular Sphere or deity.
- Vibratory charge of the magick temple through visualization by connecting into the desired energetic frequency.

The occult experimentation
- Use of the Verb and Incantations to manifest the will to achieve the purpose of the ritual.
- Mental imagery by clearly visualizing the goal as if it had already occurred.
- Make charms, talismans and other magickal items if required.
- Creation of a vortex and accumulation of energy. Increased mental power, through visualization and chanting (use of the Verb and Incantations).
- Charge and redirection of energies towards the objective to be achieved by intense visualization.

- Continuation of the mental imagery in order to strengthen the occult action on the mental plane and force the descent of the thought-form on the astral plane by projecting its emotions with intensity. Visualization of the goal as if it had already manifested itself.

Closure of the ritual

- Thanks to the deities, the God and the Goddess for their presence and help.
- Closure of the magick circle and banishing of the energies evoked by the rite.

SIXTH PART

The Grimoire of the Earth

RITUAL PRACTICE

Wᴇ have come to the most practical part of this book. Having clearly explained all the dynamics of rituals in Magick, taking into account vibratory analogies, you should now be able to compose and build your own rituals without relying on my assistance. However, to give you a starting point, I have compiled the following nine rituals so that you can practice your magick without further delay.

These rituals will be taking into account all the material that we have covered together throughout the pages of this book of witchcraft. You will also find at the beginning, before each procedure, the magickal vibratory correspondences used. If for some reason you wish to make some of your personal changes, then I urge you to do so.

Remember that the more you comply with the rules indicated in the rites that follow, the higher your chances of success will be and the faster you will be able to achieve your goals and see the fulfillment of your desires through ritual practice. Remember, dear friend, I am only your guide, and it is my duty to show you in the way forward. You are free to follow my footsteps or choose a completely different path...

That being said, you now have everything you need to achieve the most complete positive result. I wish you all the success you deserve.

Ritual of Purification and Exorcism

This ritual is very effective for all causes of purification, unhexing and exorcism, in order to purify the operator of contrary and negative energies.

Sphere of existence or Planet: Saturn
Planetary day and hour: Saturday at Saturnian hour, preferably at night
Lunar phase: Waning moon
Colors of the magick lamps: Dark purple or black
Incense Formula/magick bath: Purification and Exorcism Formula #3 + frankincense

---

On the planetary day and hour, run a bath with the coldest possible water to prepare a magnetic immersion. Unlike purifying immersions, you will instead absorb here the Saturnian vibrations in order to operate a complete exorcism.

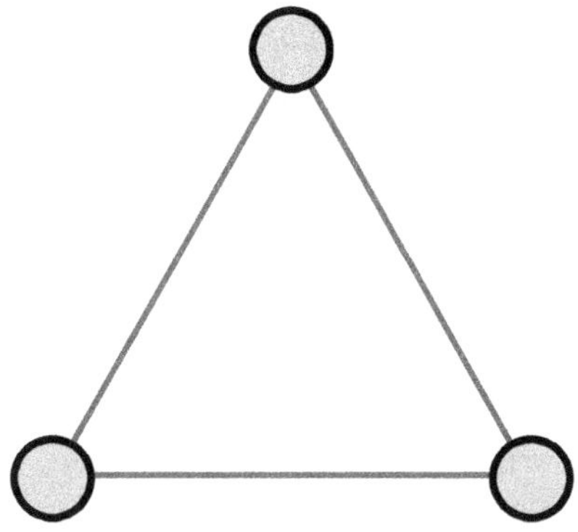

Arrange three dark purple candles, as shown in the previous figure, which you will place on a table or altar near the bathtub.

Burn your herbal composition on a charcoal pellet and place your incense burner on the table. Take a handful of the same herbs and add them into the bathwater.

Now, light the candles, then kneel down in front of your bathtub and put your hands above the surface of the water. With intense concentration and the strength of your visualization, charge the water with your desire for purification and exorcism. See the water glow with a purple aura as the charge continues.

After these preliminaries, take place in the bathtub and lie down so as to be completely covered with water. Concentrate for a moment, then recite the following incantation:

> *'By the action of the Saturnian Sphere,*
> *I open a channel to energies of pure.*
> *I cast away negativity far and near,*
> *I purify by exorcism no evil can endure.*
> *So mote it be!'*

Now visualize that your subtle bodies absorb the energy charge contained in the water and be convinced that this is actually happening in accordance with your will, transmuted and reinforced by the power of vibrations emitted by the action of incense and magickal lamps. Feel the Saturnian action taking place in you, throughout your physical, psychic and mental body. See this purifying and beneficial energy consume absolutely all the negative energies that beset you. Imagine you are a receptacle of the Saturnian vibration; that your whole being emits a luminous radiation of a dark purple color. Keep it that way and maintain your concentration. Do not forget adding some incense to the embers as needed.

After about twenty minutes of visualization, get out of the bath without drying off. Let the candles burn on their own so that the vibratory action lasts as long as possible. The purification is now complete.

Ritual of Protection

This ritual will be performed for all protection needs, whatever they may be. It will protect the operator at all levels by manifesting very high and extraordinary beneficial vibrations.

Sphere of existence or Planet: Universal Light and Sun
Planetary day and hour: Sunday at Solar hour, preferably during the day
Lunar phase: Waxing moon, full moon
Colors of the magick lamps: White and gold
Incense Formula/magick bath: Protection Formula #1 + frankincense

In your sanctuary, trace a magick circle, as you are now used to do. On your altar, in the center, place six golden candles in a hexagram shape as shown in the following figure. Finally, place one last white candle in the center of the six-pointed star. The positioning of the candles is extremely significant. This ritual will manifest the purest Universal light (use of the white candle) circled by a hexagram, symbol eminently representing the vibratory forces of the Solar Sphere (golden candles).

Start the ritual by burning your herbal composition on the embers of your incense burner. Then light the white candle representing the Universal light while saying:

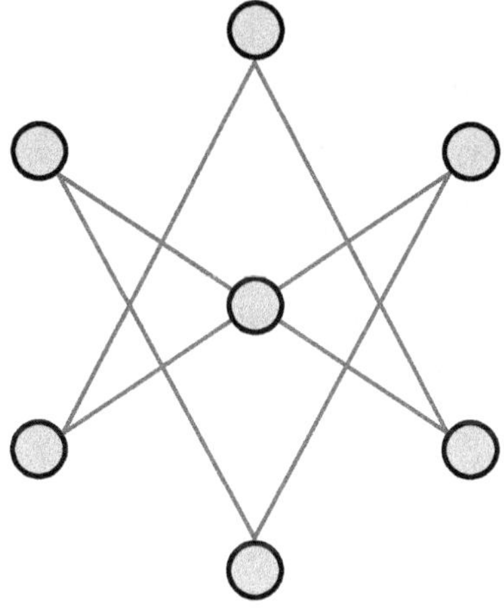

'May this symbol transcend in this sacred temple,
The Universal Light divine and evoked.
As I wear this shining mantle,
Beneficial protection I now provoke.'

Then light the six golden candles, starting at the top and continuing to the right. Say while doing so:

'I evoke in this sacred temple the Solar Sphere,
Shining through he who calls upon thee.
I consume all evil, sorrows and fear,
By fire, water, air and earth, protection is on me!'

Proceed with a meditation followed by a very intense visualization. Imagine that a beam of white light is descending from the sky as if it were drawn by the candle in the center of the hexagram. Then see this light diffusing from the flame all around you and through you. When you have this mental image clearly, do the same by visualizing a golden light being attracted by the other six candles. In summary, what you need to do is to first manifest the Universal light and then the Solar vibration. Once this work is accomplished, you should be able to see a powerful energy radiating from your altar everywhere in all directions, as if you were enlightened, almost blinded, by the luminous power of ten thousand suns.

Let yourself be bathed in this highly protective and beneficial light. Wrap yourself in this mantle of light and warmth, warmth that you might even be truly able to feel. Mentalize the fact that this light protects you and even when you no longer see it, it will remain in you and around you to perpetually protect you. Also remember to always continue feeding your incense burner all this time.

Following this work, which should last a minimum of twenty minutes, you can continue the ritual by making yourself a protective pouch. Although the mere fact of having manifested these high vibrations and visualized the action of light is amply sufficient to achieve powerful results, if you feel the need for a protective support, then take a pouch of white or yellow fabric and pour in the center a certain quantity of your herbal composition used as incense. Close the pouch and tie it with a string of the same color and wear it on you. It will be effective for a duration of about two weeks.

When you are ready to conclude this rite of protection, put your right hand on your heart and say:

'I thank the Universal and Solar light,
For the protection bestowed on me.
I am now a receptacle of shining might,
That nothing can affect, so mote it be!'

Let the candles burn by themselves so that the manifestation of the Celestial vibrations may continue. Do not close the circle until the candles are completely consumed.

Ritual of Psychism and Psychic Powers

This ritual will be performed daily to help the development of the psychic faculties of the operator. It is composed of two distinct parts. The first manifests the vibrations of the Lunar Sphere, which presides over psychic powers. The second part, meanwhile, employs a technique that stimulates the development of clairvoyance.

> *Sphere of existence or Planet:* Moon
> *Planetary day and hour:* Monday at Lunar hour, preferably at the night
> *Lunar phase:* Waxing moon, full moon
> *Colors of the magick lamps:* Silver
> *Incense Formula/magick bath:* Psychism and Psychic Powers Formula #5 + mastic

First part: psychic immersion

At the right planetary hour to practice the ritual, prepare your altar or table near your bathtub. Place nine silver candles in the shape of an enneagon. In the center, as shown in the next figure, place your cup filled with a hot decoction of Euphrasia (Eyebright) in distilled water that you have previously prepared.

Fill your bathtub with cold water and add a handful of your herbal composition. Light the candles, then kneel down and place your hands above the surface of the water. With intense concentration and the strength of your visualization, charge the water with your desire to considerably increase your psychic faculties. See the water glow with a silver aura as the charge continues.

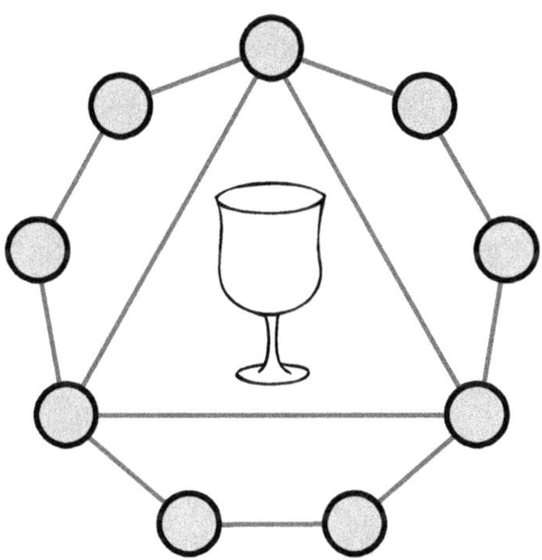

After these preliminaries, take place in the bathtub and lie down so as to be completely covered with water. Focus for a moment, then recite the call to the Lunar vibration:

'I evoke in this temple the Lunar vibrations,
Energies that govern psychic powers and visions.
May my astral centers be fully open,
By the silvery Moon, they are now awakened.'

Visualize now that your subtle bodies are absorbing the energy charge contained in the water, transmuted and reinforced by the power of vibrations emitted by the action of incense and magickal lamps. Sense the Lunar action taking place within you, throughout your physical, psychic and mental body. Feel this energy open and activate all your subtle senses. Imagine you are a receptacle of the Lunar vibration and that your psyche is active and developing; that it is becoming more and more sensitive. See your whole being emit a silver-colored glow of light.

Continue this way and maintain your concentration. Do not forget to add some incense on the embers as needed. After about twenty minutes, get out of the bathtub without drying off. The action of the Lunar Sphere is completed.

Second part: the activation of clairvoyance

Take two cotton balls and immerse them in the cup to soak them thoroughly with the Euphrasia decoction, which should now be warm. Next, place the cottons on your closed eyes and lie down for a period of about fifteen to thirty minutes. While you relax, activate your clairvoyance through visualization by following the subsequent step.

Feel that from now on; your eyes acquire the properties of clairvoyance, as is the case with Universal light. This light is unique, it illuminates and pierces all that exists; it lifts the veil on all that is covered; neither time nor space can stand in the way of this grandiose light. And so it is for your eyes. They are now able to see through everything.

When you have concluded this step, after thirty minutes, the ritual will be completed. Let the candles burn on their own so that the Lunar vibrations remains. You can repeat this entire ritual or the second part only as often as you like.

Ritual of Money and Wealth

This ritual will be practiced over a period of seven consecutive days to attract influences and vibrations of a monetary order, money, material wealth and financial prosperity.

Sphere of existence or Planet: Jupiter
Planetary day and hour: Thursday at Jupiterian hour
Lunar phase: Waxing moon until the full moon
Colors of the magick lamps: Royal blue
Incense Formula/magick bath: Money and Wealth Formula #6

Before starting the ritual, set up your altar with eleven royal blue candles, as shown in the following figure. In addition, have a large bowl of cold water or your cauldron at hand, as well as your usual magick tools.

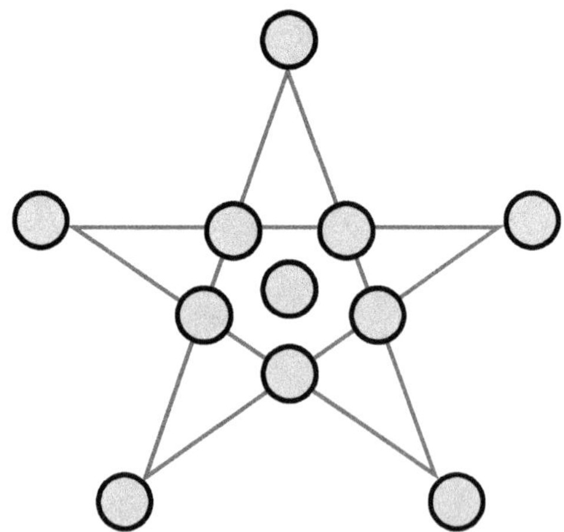

Draw a magick circle using your athame. Then, once the circle is consecrated, it will be time to manifest the Jupiterian vibration in your temple with the help of fumigation and lamps. To do this, throw a good amount of incense on the embers of your censer, remembering to always feed it as needed, throughout the ritual.

Finally, light up the five candles on the outside, those standing at each point of the pentagram. You will use the other candles in the following days.

Focus on the frequency of the Jupiter Sphere. Through visualization, bring down a bluish light which, when touching the water of the cauldron, will diffuse everywhere inside your magick circle. You can, for example, suck this light out of your breath. Imagine this luminous flux becoming progressively charged with the vibration of material wealth. Feel you are immersed in financial prosperity.

After a few minutes of concentration, place your hands above the surface of the water in the cauldron. With intense visualization, charge the water with your desire to increase your financial situation and see the water glow with a blue aura as the charge continues. Afterwards, ask for abundance as follows:

'By grace of Heaven and Jupiter influences,
I am granted monetary abundance.
Being prosperous is my aim,
Manifest! Manifest! Earthly wealth I obtain!'

Immerse your hands in the water and visualize how your subtle bodies absorb this energetic charge, just like a magick bath would. Feel the Jupiterian action operating in you and bringing the desired changes. After a short period of time, remove your hands. You can stay in the energy contained in the circle for as long as you want. The first phase of the ritual is now over. Let the candles burn completely.

Repeating the call

For the next six days, at the same planetary hour, you will light one of the six candles on your altar and burn the incense. Save the central candle for the last day. You will then manifest your will and desire by the following incantation:

> *'By grace of Heaven and Jupiter influences,*
> *I am granted monetary abundance.*
> *Being prosperous is my aim,*
> *Manifest! Manifest! Earthly wealth I obtain!*
> *O Jupiterian vibration manifest yourself in me.*
> *So money and wealth hasten. So mote it be!'*

For a few minutes, visualize and meditate on your goal to achieve, which is to obtain monetary abundance. Visualize yourself as if you were already living in this wealth. See and project your desire as if it had already manifested itself. After a period of time, leave the candle unattended; you can now let the action work for you without your presence.

Repeat the call the next day and so on, at the rate of one candle per day. Until the whole ritual is completed, avoid moving the candles on your altar.

Ritual of Work and Social Elevation

This ritual will allow the operator to attract and manifest vibrations that are very beneficial and propitious for all that concerns employment, work relations and personal elevation on a social level.

Sphere of existence or Planet: Jupiter
Planetary day and hour: Thursday at Jupiterian hour
Lunar phase: Waxing moon until the full moon
Colors of the magick lamps: Royal blue
Incense Formula/magick bath: Work and Social Elevation Formula #1

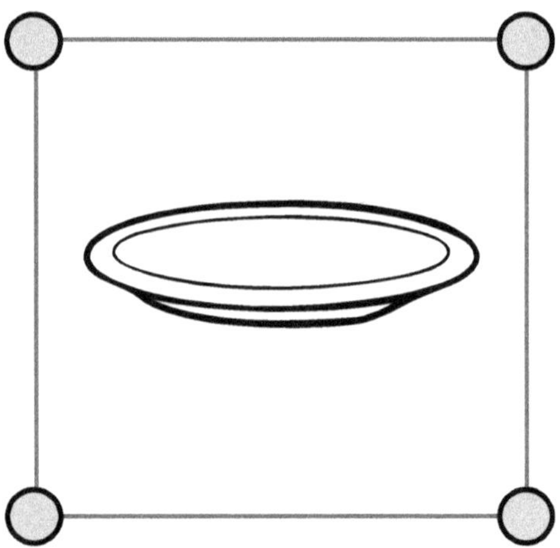

Arrange your altar as usual, on a Thursday, at the chosen Jupiterian hour, and place four royal blue candles in the shape of a square, as shown in the figure. You will have previously divided the incense into seven equal parts that you will burn at the rate of one portion per day. In the center of this figure, place a plate containing a generous amount of Vaseline[4]. The latter will be used to compose a magick ointment that you will apply at the end of the ritual.

Begin the ceremony by tracing a magick circle with your athame. Next, evoke the Jupiterian vibrations by burning the incense and lighting the candles. Concentrate for a moment, then raise your arms and express your will with these words:

'In this temple, Jupiter I call your light,
Manifest my desire day and night!
Be favorable for (stipulate your desire),
This will of me I want to see. So mote it be!'

Now visualize your desire very intensely and project yourself into the coveted situation, as if it had already manifested itself. Perform this mental work for several consecutive minutes. Throughout this process, continue to feel the Jupiterian action within you, at all levels, and all around you... great changes are about to take place!

Later, when you feel the moment is right, take a handful of your herbs (previously reduced to powder) used for

---

4   Petroleum jelly (or Vaseline), readily available commercially can be substituted with a neutral cosmetic ointment base or natural, odorless skin cream.

fumigation and toss them on your plate containing the petroleum jelly. Using your hands or a wooden spoon, mix everything together to obtain a homogeneous composition. Thus, prepare your ointment while visualizing and intensely charging it with your will through your desire for employment or your social situation (desire which was clearly stated in the previous call to the Jupiterian forces). It is very important to charge the ointment properly so it becomes operational.

The magick ointment will produce the effect of harmonizing the energetic flow by acting directly on your etheric body. In this way your aura will become charged and magnetized with the desired vibration tending towards the accomplishment of your goal. The use of such a magickal accessory produces admirable and surprising effects.

When your mixture is ready for use, lift up your ritual robe and anoint your seven energy centers, namely: at the base of your sex; at the level of your lower abdomen; on your solar plexus; at the level of your heart; at the throat; on the third eye in between your eyebrows; and finally, above your head. Instantly feel the magickal action operating and transmitting the charge to your etheric body. Continue to visualize your fulfilled desire until an entire section of the candles has been consumed. Then extinguish them with your thumb and index finger. The first part of the ritual is now complete.

Repeating the call

For the next six days, at the Jupiterian hour, relight the candles for one new section per day and burn a fumigation of the same incense. Focus on the goal pursued, then recite the call once again:

'In this temple, Jupiter I call your light,
Manifest my desire day and night!
Be favorable for (stipulate your desire),
This will of me I want to see. So mote it be!'

Finally, anoint yourself with your magick ointment and continue to visualize your desire until the candle section has completely burned. On the last day, let the candles burn out completely.

Ritual of Love and Feelings

The following ritual will be performed to considerably magnetize the aura of the operator so as to make him much more magnetic towards the opposite sex. It will provoke and attract love and sensual desires.

Love causes and everything related to desires, sexuality and sensuality are intimately connected to the Cosmic Element of Fire. It is for this reason that, when a situation of this order hardly leads to a given desire, it is due to the fact that this Element is either disordered in the person suffering from these deficiencies or because it does not manifest itself as it should, since there is an elemental imbalance in the structure of being. To rectify the situation, this ritual will manifest and activate in the operator the fiery vibration in order to charge and magnetize his etheric body, thereby making it as attractive as a magnet.

Sphere of existence or Planet: Fire Element, Mars or Venus
Planetary day and hour: Man — Tuesday at Martian hour
Planetary day and hour: Woman — Friday at Venusian hour
Lunar phase: Waxing moon until the full moon
Colors of the magick lamps: Red
Incense Formula/magick bath: Love and Feelings Formula #2 (for man), Formula #1 (for woman)

Depending on whether you are male or female, you will practice this ritual on a Tuesday or Friday, at the planetary hour prescribed above. Set up your altar table with your usual magick tools. Next, place six red candles, as shown in the following figure.

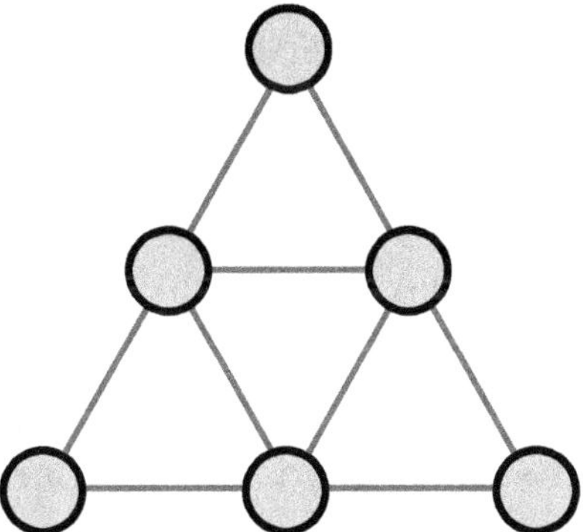

Trace a magick circle using your athame. Then activate the vibratory manifestation of Fire by burning incense on the embers of your censer. Use the formula for your gender. Light the three candles that make up the outer triangle only. The rest will be burned during the recall.

Now focus on your desire to become magnetic in order to attract to yourself love and sensual desires. Visualize that your whole being is filled with a bright red light that radiates in all directions: the Fire Element. The vibratory action of the latter charges your aura with your most intense desire. Feel having become a magnetic center attracting sensual pleasures, erotic desires, love passions, etc.

Maintain your focus and visualize your goal over a period of at least fifteen to thirty minutes. When your concentration begins to wane, invoke the Sphere of Power one last time as follows:

'By the (Martian or Venusian) Fire that burns in me,
Flames of (Mars or Venus) radiate all around to see!
By the (Martian or Venusian) Fire of impulsions,
Flames of (Mars or Venus) create passions!
(Martian or Venusian) Fire that burns and ignite,
I radiate and people become under my might!
I am irresistible, people come to me,
I call for love, so mote it be!'

The first part of the ritual is now completed. Add incense to the embers and let the candles burn completely.

Repeating the call

For the next three days, at the same planetary hour, manifest the action of Fire again by repeating the same procedure with the difference that you will burn only one red candle, and obviously, the same incense.

You can also practice in conjunction with this ritual a magick bath immediately after the ceremony or make and charge an ointment using a petroleum jelly base as well as the same herbs used in the fumigation, which will have been previously reduced to a fine powder. This ointment will have the effect of magnetizing you even more and perpetuating the magickal action and emission of the Fire Element.

)O(

Ritual of Health, Peace and Well-being

This ritual was developed to meet the majority of health, peace and well-being needs. Depending on the precise action one wishes to obtain, the operator will use the most appropriate mix of herbs by referring to the *plant compositions for magick baths and incense* at the end of the third part of this work. This ritual will make use of formula #4, which generates excellent vibrations promoting healing and general health.

> *Sphere of existence or Planet:* Sun
> *Planetary day and hour:* Sunday at the Solar hour, during the day
> *Lunar phase:* Waxing moon until the full moon
> *Colors of the magick lamps:* Gold
> *Incense Formula/magick bath:* Health, Peace and Well-Being Formula #4 + frankincense

Begin the preparations for the ritual by setting up your altar with your usual magick tools; candles and candlesticks, incense burner, athame, etc. You will also have divided your candles into seven equal parts in order to burn only one part per day. Next, place the golden candles in the shape of a Solar hexagram, in addition to a white candle, in the center, following the figure on the next page.

Trace a magick circle using your athame. Then activate the vibratory manifestation of the Solar Sphere through incense and light, by adding incense on the embers of your incense burner and lighting the candles. Start with the upper candle, then continue to the right, ending with the white candle in the center.

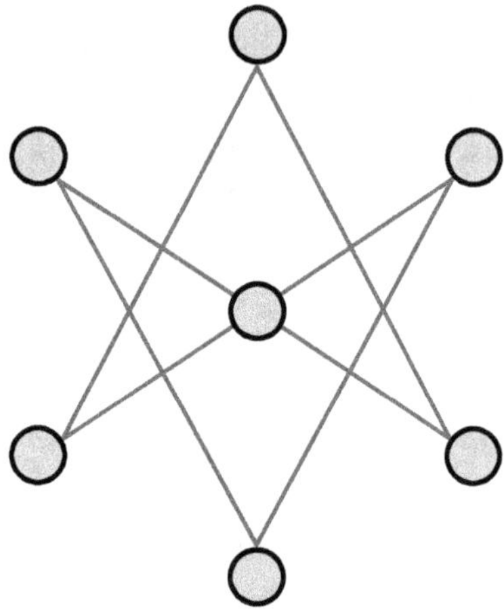

Concentrate on your desire for health or healing, or even both. Visualize that your magickal temple and your entire being are filled with the purest and brightest golden light; that light penetrates you and radiates in all directions. Visualize that the vibratory action of the Solar Sphere is charging your aura with your most intense desire. Feel you are a magnetic and an attractive center of all the beneficial and conducive vibrations to health and healing.

Maintain your focus and visualize the goal to be attained for a period of at least fifteen to thirty minutes or until a section of candles has burned completely. Then extinguish them with your thumb and index finger. Thank the Solar energies for its action. The first part of the ritual is now over.

Repeating the call

For the next six days, at the same planetary hour, manifest the Solar action again by repeating the same procedure, for the remaining time of a candle section, and always with a fumigation of the same incense. On the last day, let the candles be consumed completely.

You can also practice in conjunction with this ritual a magick bath immediately after the ceremony or make and charge an ointment using a petroleum jelly base as well as the same herbs used in the fumigation, which have been previously reduced to a fine powder. This ointment will produce the effect of magnetizing you even more and prolonging the magickal action and emission of the Solar Sphere favorable to your desire.

Ritual of Strength and Power

This ritual was developed to evoke very strong Martian vibratory currents, which govern, among other things, strength and power. Depending on the precise action one wishes to obtain, the operator will use the most suitable herb combination by referring to the *plant compositions for magick baths and incense*. The ritual will make use of formula #7 (except the dill whose Fire is Venusian), which generates excellent vibrations favoring power, strength as well as courage in the person who uses it.

Sphere of existence or planetary: Fire and Mars
Planetary day and hour: Tuesday at Martian hour, during the day or the night
Lunar phase: Waxing moon until the full moon
Colors of the magick lamps: Red
Incense Formula/magick bath: Strength and Power Formula #7 + dragon's blood

---

Before starting the ritual, position your altar with five red candles in the shape of a pentagram that you will have previously divided into seven equal parts in order to consume one part per day. In addition, have a large bowl of cold water or your cauldron handy, as well as your usual magickal tools.

Draw a magick circle using your athame. Then manifest the Martian vibration in your temple with a fumigation and magick lamps. To do this, toss a good amount of incense on the embers of your incense burner, remembering to always feed as needed, then light the candles.

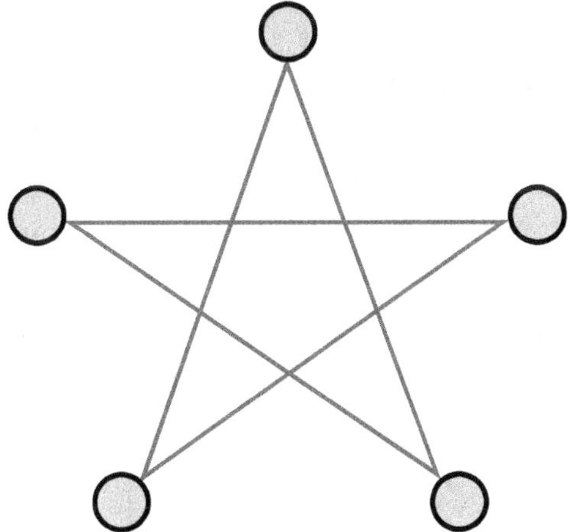

Now focus on the frequency of the Martian Sphere. Through visualization, bring down an intense red light that will diffuse everywhere inside your sanctuary. You can, for example, suck this light in via conscious skin breathing. Imagine this luminous flux getting charged with increasingly qualities of strength and power. Feel yourself becoming almost overloaded with energy.

After a few minutes of concentration, place your hands above the surface of the cauldron water. With intense visualization, charge the water with your desire and see the water glow with a reddish aura as the charge continues. Then ask to acquire the Martian qualities as follows:

'By Martian Fire I charge and attract,
Strength and power it is now a fact.
Courage and might now vibrate in me,
Martian Fire manifest, so mote it be!'

Immerse your hands in the water and visualize how your etheric body absorbs the energetic charge. Perceive the action taking place in you and effecting the desired changes. Know that Martian Fire is transmitted in your body and brings you the requested qualities. After a short period of time, remove your hands. You can stay in the energy contained in the circle as long as you want.

Now, take a handful of your herbs (previously reduced to powder) used for fumigation and, using your hands or a wooden spoon, combine them with a petroleum jelly base until you obtain a homogeneous composition. Accordingly, prepare a magick ointment while visualizing and intensely charging it with your will through your desire. It is extremely important to charge the ointment properly to make it operational.

The magick ointment will cause the effect of harmonizing the energy flow by acting directly on your etheric body. In this way your aura will become charged and magnetized with the Martian vibration, which will manifest strength, courage and power.

When your mixture is ready for use, lift up your ritual robe and cover your seven energy centers, that is: at the base of your sex; at the level of your lower abdomen; on your solar plexus; at the level of your heart; at the throat; on the third eye in between your eyebrow arches; and finally, above your head. Immediately feel the magickal action operating and conveying the charge to your etheric body. Light the candles until a whole section has burned entirely. Next turn them off with your thumb and index finger. The first part of the ritual is now complete.

If you do not want to use the magick ointment, you can always, as a substitute, make a pouch of red fabric with the same herbs previously charged with your will. You will wear the pouch around your neck for a period of two weeks.

Repeating the call

For the next six days, at the same planetary hour, manifest again the action of the Martian Fire by repeating the identical procedure, for the duration of a candle section, and as always with a fumigation of the same incense. The last day, let the candles burn out completely.

)O(

Ritual of Prosperity, Luck and Success

The following ritual has been designed to manifest specific vibrations that promote success on several levels, opening a channel to higher energies so as to allow them flow into the operator.

There are certain Spheres of existence and planets conducive to prosperity and success. Let us mention in particular the Cosmic Element of the Earth: Malkuth, to obtain abundance and wealth at the level of the terrestrial and material plane, the Sphere of Jupiter: Chesed, which is very favorable to commercial activities and for business, the Sphere of Mercury: Hod, to attract customers, etc.

However, this ritual will align with the Solar Sphere, which generally also dominates success, luck, glory and fame at all levels. If your needs become more specific, then you can, after a brief in-depth study of the correspondences, modify the ritual accordingly to the Sphere governing the precise area in which you wish to achieve success.

Sphere of existence or Planet: Sun

Planetary day and hour: Sunday at the Solar hour, during the day

Lunar phase: Waxing moon until the full moon

Colors of the magick lamps: Gold

Incense Formula/magick bath: Prosperity, Luck and Success Formula #1 + pontifical

---

The first consideration to take before going any further, and what I strongly recommend, is the possibility of first practicing a ritual using the Saturnian Sphere in order to carry out a complete purification. By initially performing an exorcism, you will be able to banish all influences that undermine your success by spreading it with pitfalls and bad luck. Once the path is clear for success and the shackles have been removed, it would be much easier for you to manifest the energies and vibrations favorable in obtaining prosperity, success and luck.

Practice a magnetic immersion using the Saturnian Sphere or perform the complete ritual of *Purification and Exorcism*, cited at the beginning of this chapter, to get rid of obstacles and all contrary vibrations.

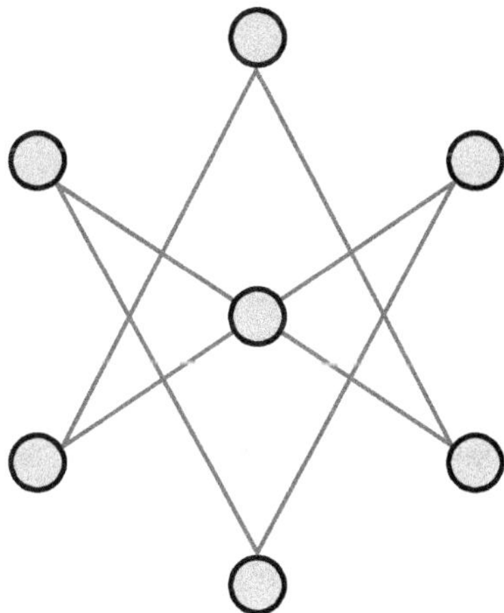

Having done so, on the planetary day and hour of the Sun, lay on your altar six golden candles, divided into seven equal parts, arranged in the form of a hexagram. You will finally place a seventh white candle in the center.

Trace a magick circle using your athame, then activate the vibratory manifestation of the Solar Sphere by tossing incense on the embers of your censer and by lighting the candles. Start with the upper candle, then continue to the right, to finish with the white candle in the center.

Now focus on your desire in a very intense way. Visualize that your magickal temple and your whole being are filled with the purest and brightest golden light there is; this light penetrates you and radiates in all directions. Visualize the vibratory action of the Solar Sphere is charging your aura with your desire for prosperity, success, luck, etc. Feel with all your strength that you are now a magnetized center attracting all the vibrations that are beneficial and auspicious in achieving your ultimate goal. Maintain your concentration and visualize that you are enticing what you want most for a period of at least fifteen minutes.

Then, after this intense mental imagery, make a pouch of golden, yellow or white fabric including the same herbs used for fumigation. Charge these herbs with your will knowing that this pouch is a perfect natural magnet that will vibrate the Solar Sphere and attract prosperity, luck and success, etc. Wear this magick pouch around your neck. This will be effective for a period of two weeks.

At last, thank the Solar power for its action. Let the candles burn until an entire section has been consumed. Then extinguish them with your thumb and index finger. The first part of the ritual is now concluded.

Repeating the call

For the next six days, at the same planetary hour, manifest the Solar action again by repeating the same procedure, for the length of a candle section, and always with a fumigation of the same incense. On the last day let the candles completely consumed themselves.

THE VIRTUES OF HERBS, PLANTS & ESSENTIAL OILS

TOGETHER, we have seen throughout this book the importance of energies and how vital it was to take these vibratory frequencies into account to carry out a successful magickal operation. We know all the more that when we practice a ritual, it is essential to align ourselves with these vibrations so as to create in our magickal sanctuary a channel allowing the manifestation of a given Sphere of existence. Consequently, know that this vibratory rule affects absolutely everything that exists, including for herbs, plants and all botanical species. Each emits a signal which is in agreement or if you prefer, in analogy or sympathy with a planetary and elemental Sphere. Now, when the time comes to compose your own herbal compositions of incense, powders and magick baths, you will, of course, always have to take into account these correspondences so that your mixtures reflect and vibrate in perfect harmony with a higher Sphere and therefore they can represent and manifest your desire and will.

Here is an exhaustive chart with more than 175 herbs, plants and essential oils as well as their vibratory correspondences and magickal properties. Not to mention the fact that you will be capable to utilize abundantly the compositions given at the end of the third part of this book, by consulting all these simple plants, you will be able to develop new mixtures and formulas for all your needs in practical magick.

Index of Properties and Correspondences

Herbs, Plants & Oils	Spheres	Elements	Magickal Properties
A			
Acacia	Sun	Fire/Water/Air	Protection, health, healing, spiritual elevation, inspiration, high clairvoyance.
Agrimony	Jupiter	Water	Progress, prosperity, justice, zombie magick, reversal.
Alfalfa	Venus	Fire	Prosperity in matters of love.
Allspice	Mars	Fire	Attack and defense, protection, power, strength and virility.
Almond tree	Mercury	Water	Accentuates and facilitates mental work, premonitions, wisdom.
Aloe	Moon	Water/Air	Black Magick, lower astral, demons, prosperity, money, wealth, luck.
Amaranth	Saturn	Water	Brings help to the dying and deceased, funeral rites.
Angelica	Sun	Fire/Water/Air	Guard against spells and love passions, promotes spiritual evolution, health and healing, provides harmony and peace, intuition, breaks love spells.

Anise	Moon	Water/Air	Protects and calms the psyche, psychic receptivity, clairvoyance, protection against nightmares, memory.
Apple Tree	Sun	Fire/Water/Air	Health and healing, peace and harmony, luck.
Apricot	Venus	Fire	Promotes love, desires and brings sensuality.
Arbutus Andrachne	Moon	Water/Air	Fast healing, restores the etheric body wonderfully, pregnant women, gestation, sleep, the dying.
Ash	Earth	4 Elements	Attracts money and material wealth.
Avocado	Venus	Fire	Aphrodisiac, provides a very strong sexuality and vitality, love and romantic luck, encounters.
B			
Basil	Sun Jupiter Mercury	Fire/Water/Air	One of the most beneficial herbs, promotes the achievement of higher spiritual psychic faculties, protection, mental clarity, against anxiety.
Beech	Saturn	Water	Provides help to the dying and the deceased, promotes the remission of karmic debts.
Bergamot	Mercury	Water	Financial prosperity, attracts money.
Birch	Venus	Fire	Helps with marriages, promotes and protects sentimental life, love, communication with fairies.
Birdsfoot Trefoil	Moon	Water/Air	Develops clairvoyance, calms and purifies the psyche.
Bitter Dock	Jupiter	Water	Provides financial prosperity and attracts money.
Blessed Thistle	Mars	Fire	Against monetary losses, provides power, breaks bad spells, makes wishes come true.

Bloodroot	Mars	Fire	Protection from thieves, reverses spells, defense and purification.
Blueberry	Venus	Fire	Confers protection against love passions and establishes emotional peace in relationships.
Boxwood	Sun	Fire/Water/Air	Confers very great protection, health and healing, promotes inspiration.
Buckthorn	Saturn	Water	Help during trials and obtaining justice.
Burdock	Venus	Fire	Attracts love and banishes negativity in couples.
C			
Cabbage	Moon	Water/Air	Purifying agent of the psyche.
Camellia	Moon	Water/Air	Brings joy and wealth.
Camphor	Moon Mercury Neptune	Water	Great purifying agent, purifies the psyche and dwelling places.
Caraway	Mercury	Water	Increases the intellect and protects against love passions.
Cardamom	Venus	Fire	Brings strong feelings, promotes art and creativity, attraction and love, sexuality.
Carob	Mars	Fire	Provides protection, courage and power.
Cascara Sagrada	Sun	Fire/Water/Air	Brings financial prosperity.
Catnip	Venus	Fire	Against bad luck, feline magick, familiars, happiness.

Cedar	Sun	Fire/Water/Air	Protection, purification, health and healing, inspiration and harmony.
Celery	Saturn	Water	Protects and purifies, provides wisdom.
Chamomile	Sun	Fire/Water/Air	Healing and health, provides inspiration and protection, purification, meditation and tranquility.
Chickweed	Moon	Water/Air	Charms of illusions and invisibility.
Chicory	Mars	Fire	Keeps enemies away, provides strength and courage.
Chili Pepper	Mars	Fire	Attack and defense, protection, strength and virility.
Cinnamon	Venus	Fire	Brings strong feelings, promotes art and creativity, attraction, love, sexuality.
Cinquefoil	Mars	Fire	Activity and mental protection, protects against dark and negative thoughts.
Citrus	Moon	Water/Air	Excellent protection and purification agent.
Clove	Venus	Fire	Purifies emotions and soothes conflicts, exorcism, remove spells, thwarts attacks.
Clover	Saturn	Water	Keeps away painful trials and purifies vibrations.
Columbine	Venus	Fire	Aphrodisiac, attracts love and passions, provokes desires and eroticism.
Comfrey	Saturn	Water	Travel, security/safety.
Coriander	Mars	Fire	Sexual desires, confers strength and courage.

Couchgrass	Jupiter	Water	Wealth, respect in social causes.
Cucumber	Moon	Water	To be used to counter infertility.
Cumin	Mars	Fire	Sexual desires, confers strength and courage.
Cyclamen	Moon	Water	Soothes passions and protects the home.
Cypress	Saturn	Water	Provides help to the dying and the deceased, promotes the remission of karmic debts.
D			
Daisy	Sun	Fire/Water/Air	Promotes deep feelings and inspiration.
Damiana	Venus	Fire	Attracts love, passions and romantic relationships, promotes sexuality.
Dandelion	Mercury	Water	Provides luck on the material plane and attracts money, calls the Spirits.
Devil's Claw	Mars	Fire	Exorcism, love, luck, protection against the Devil.
Devil's Shoestring	Jupiter	Water	Luck in gambling, helps to find a job.
Dill	Venus	Fire	Aphrodisiac, love, attraction, magnetism, vitality, sexuality, intimate connections and romantic relationships.
E			
Echinacea	Sun	Fire/Water/Air	Healing and health, purification, strengthens spells.
Elderberry	Venus	Fire	Protects against love spells and the passionate causes of love.

Elm	Saturn	Water	Favorable for the obtaining of justice and truth, ceases rumors and gossip.
Eucalyptus	Sun	Fire/Water/Air	Protection, purification, healing and health, harmony, success, luck, inspiration.
Eyebright	Sun	Fire/Water/Air	Confers pure clairvoyance, protection, healing and health, success, inspiration, wisdom, mental powers.
F			
Fennel	Mercury	Water	Attracts monetary and money.
Fenugreek	Moon	Water/Air	Confers material prosperity.
Fern	Sun	Fire/Water/Air	Brings success, victory, glory and fame.
Flax	Sun	Fire/Water/Air	High clairvoyance, psychic powers, luck, protection, health and healing.
Fumitory	Saturn	Water	Exorcise and unhexing, protection and purification.
G			
Galangal	Mars	Fire	Breaks evil spells, provides strength and protection.
Gardenia	Sun	Fire/Water/Air	Health and healing, brings strong feelings and inspiration.
Garlic	Mars	Fire	Strength and power against adversity, purification, exorcises vibrations.
Gentian	Venus	Fire	Against love and emotional passions, promotes honest feelings.
Geranium	Venus	Fire	Against love and emotional passions, promotes honest feelings.

Ginger	Mars	Fire	Sexual potency, vitality, strength and protection.
Ginkgo	Earth	4 Elements	Prosperity and material wealth, vitality, concentration, mental clarity, inner balance.
Ginseng	Earth	4 Elements	Prosperity wealth, sexual potency and vitality.
Gorse	Mars	Fire	Strength, combat, power, protection against adversity and sorcery, social elevation, prosperity, competition.
H			
Hawthorn	Moon	Water/Air	Favorable for marriages and protects the couples and their home, brings fertility and cheerfulness.
Hazel	Mercury	Water	Promotes mental activity, calm and soothes, peace, relaxation.
Heather	Moon	Water/Air	Brings protection to children and the home, rain, immortality, beauty.
Heliotrope	Sun	Fire/Water/Air	Inspiration, luck, health and healing, protection.
Hibiscus	Sun	Fire/Water/Air	Strong feelings, divination.
Honeysuckle	Jupiter	Water	Protection and social elevation, promotes employment.
Hop	Mars	Fire	Protection, visions and healing.
Horsetail	Saturn	Water	Charm-snake, brings fertility.
Hyacinth	Jupiter	Water	Promotes money, work and social elevation.

Hyssop	Sun	Fire/Water/Air	Very high clairvoyance, protection, purification, luck.
I			
Iris	Moon	Water/Air	Promotes the development of clairvoyance, divination and dreams, purifies the psyche.
J			
Jasmine	Venus	Fire	Love and passions, develops psychic powers.
Juniper	Sun	Fire/Water/Air	Provides protection, promotes luck and inspiration, healing, purification.
L			
Lady's Mantle	Moon	Water/Air	Protects from anxieties, restores the psyche, vampirism, incubus, succubus.
Laurel	Sun	Fire/Water/Air	Protection, health and healing, inspiration, reverses bad luck.
Lavender	Moon	Water/Air	Extreme protection of the psyche, provides protection, develops clairvoyance, happiness, peace, purification.
Lemon Balm	Moon	Water/Air	Protects the psyche and the household.
Licorice	Venus	Fire	Love, romantic relationships and sincere feelings, sexuality, fidelity, bonding charms.
Lily	Moon Mercury Venus	Fire/Water/Air	Confers great power on the earthy plane, provides protection and purifies vibrations.
Lily of the Valley	Mercury	Water	Attracts money and stimulates intellectual faculties.

Linden	Jupiter	Water	Chases away melancholy and brings joy and bliss.
Lingonberry	Venus	Fire	Protection against love passions, emotional peace, return of affection, breaking love enchantments.
M			
Mandrake	Mercury Saturn	Water	The mystical plant of choice; protection, healing and health, money, fertility, divination, romantic and social relationships, eternal love.
Maple	Jupiter	Water	Wealth, money, work and sociability.
Marigold	Sun	Fire/Water/Air	Soothes passions, provides calm and harmony, popularity.
Marjoram	Moon	Water/Air	Purifies and protects the psyche, promotes peace and mental relaxation.
Marsh mallow	Moon	Water/Air	Helps to develop clairvoyance, protects the home, psyche, protection, comfort.
Mauve	Moon	Water/Air	Purification and protection of the psyche, promotes mental peace and detachment.
Mayweed	Sun	Fire/Water/Air	Attracts extremely beneficial vibrations.
Mint	Mercury	Water	Develops psychic powers and mental activity, wisdom.
Mistletoe	Sun	Fire/Water/Air	Protection, purification, luck, health and healing.
Mugwort	Sun	Fire/Water/Air	Promotes clairvoyance and clear visions, astral projections, inspiration.
Mullein	Saturn	Water	Brings dreams, health, exorcism, strength, sleep.

Mustard	Mars	Fire	Attack and defense, ward off enemies and confers protection.
N			
Nettle	Mars	Fire	Keeps enemies away, confers protection and strength.
O			
Oak	Earth	The 4 Elements	Wealth, grants health, healing and vitality, protection, druidic magick, wisdom, fertility.
Oats	Venus	Fire	Material abundance, prosperity, strength and vitality.
Olive Tree	Sun	Fire/Water/Air	Brings wisdom, confers protection, health and healing, luck and inspiration.
Onion	Mars	Fire	Provides protection and purifies vibrations.
Orange Tree	Sun	Fire/Water/Air	Attracts high beneficial vibrations, provides luck.
Orchid	Venus	Fire	Promotes love, loving passions and eroticism.
Oregano	Mercury	Water	Strengthens the mind, brings luck and freedom, protects from love passions.
P			
Pansy	Moon	Water/Air	Protection, purification, promotes strong feelings.
Parsley	Mercury	Water	Luck and prosperity.
Passiflora	Venus	Fire	Provides peace and tranquility, friendship and love.

Pear Tree	Venus	Fire	Love and romantic relationships, promotes the expression of strong and deep feelings.
Pennyroyal	Venus	Fire	Peace, protection against the evil eye, tranquility.
Pepper Tree	Mars	Fire	Attack and defense, protection, power, strength and virility.
Periwinkle	Moon	Water/Air	Promotes love and marriages and protects them.
Pine	Mars	Fire	Attack and defense, protection, power, strength and virility.
Pineapple	Sun	Fire/Water/Air	Provides luck, prosperity, splendor and money.
Pistachio	Mercury	Water	Provides material luck and attracts money.
Plantain	Venus	Fire	Protection and strength.
Poplar	Sun	Fire/Water/Air	Illuminates the mind and promotes its activity.
Poppy	Moon	Water/Air	Fertility, sleep, invisibility.
Primrose	Venus	Fire	Love, procures great torrid passions.
R			
Raspberry Bush	Moon	Water/Air	Provides home protection and fertility.
Rhubarb	Venus	Fire	Love, romantic relationships and sincere feelings.
Rose	Sun	Fire/Water/Air	One of the most wonderful herbs, attracts a very high beneficial vibrations, love, harmony and strong feelings, purity and purification.

Rosemary	Sun	Fire/Water/Air	Protection, purification, lucidity, luck and peace, youth, healing.
Rowan	Sun	Fire/Water/Air	Generates very positive and beneficial vibrations.
Rue	Mercury	Water	Calms and soothes nervousness, attracts money, wisdom, mental powers.
S			
Saffron	Sun	Fire/Water/Air	Wealth, success, glory, luck, health and healing.
Sage	Sun	Fire/Water/Air	Protection, health and healing, prosperity and luck, wisdom, wishes, endurance, protection from Spirits, immortality.
Sandalwood	Sun	Fire/Water/Air	Purification and holiness, brings harmony and peace, spirituality, wishes, protection.
Sarsaparilla	Jupiter	Water	Work and employment, wealth, social elevation.
Sassafras	Moon	Water/Air	Confers a quick but short-lived stroke of luck.
Savory	Sun	Fire/Water/Air	Longevity, health and healing, luck and protection.
Scabious	Venus	Fire	Stirs up love and love passions, feelings.
Senna	Mercury	Water	Good for love charms.
Sesame	Sun	Fire/Water/Air	Generates very positives and beneficial vibrations.
Shepherd's Purse	Moon	Water/Air	Helps develop psychic powers.
Skullcap	Saturn	Water	Fidelity, peace.

Name	Planet	Element	Virtues
St. John's Wort	Sun	Fire/Water/Air	Protection, health and healing, luck and inspiration.
Solomon's Seal	Saturn	Water	Brings stability at different levels, invocation of Spirits.
Strawberry Tree	Moon	Water/Air	Provides home protection and fertility.
Sweet Alyssum	Sun	Fire/Water/Air	Freedom and movement, joy and cheerfulness, development of human relationships.
T			
Tarragon	Venus	Fire	Attracts love, passions and romantic relationships.
Tea Tree	Sun	Fire/Water/Air	Increases mental activity and provides luck.
Thyme	Sun	Fire/Water/Air	Attracts money, wealth, finances, protection, health and healing, purification.
Tulip	Mercury	Water	Calms and relaxes the affective life and protects against love passions.
Turmeric	Sun	Fire/Water/Air	Provides protection, harmony and peace, health and healing.
V			
Valerian	Sun	Fire/Water/Air	Against depressions, calm, relax, health and healing relaxation, purification, constraint.
Vanilla	Venus	Fire	Stirs up sensual desires and attracts love and eroticism.
Vervain	Venus	Fire	Love, calms and purifies emotions, increases feelings and creativity, youth, purification.
Vetivert	Mars	Fire	Sexual attraction and desires, potency, vitality and strength.

Violet	Venus	Fire	Arouses sensual desires, attracts love, loving passions and eroticism.
W			
Willow	Moon	Water/Air	Divination, dreams, psyche, healing, protection.
Witch-Hazel	Saturn	Water	Chastity, protection, luck.
Woodruff	Mars	Fire	Attack and defense, victory, protection and purification.
Wormwood	Mars	Fire	Dissolve psychic larvae, exorcism, purification, protection, communication with Spirits, full moon magick.
Y			
Yarrow	Venus	Fire	Exorcism, unhexing, purification, protection, love and love desires, friendship.
Yerba Santa	Mars	Fire	Beauty, protection, power, might and strength.
Yohimbe	Mars	Fire	Aphrodisiac, sexual desires, raises passions and desires.
Yucca	Mars	Fire	Beauty, healing, protection, psychic powers.